The Meanderings of a Serial Goat Keeper

Vivienne Bennett

To Julie

Best wishes from Viv x

V. Bennett

Copyright

The Meanderings of a Serial Goat Keeper

Third Edition 2021

©Vivienne Bennett 2021.

All rights reserved. The text of this publication, or any part of, may not be reproduced in full or in part without express written permission from the author.

ISBN 781 291 024 210

for

my children

Contents

Foreword by Johanna Seymour Tavernor
Secretary for the English Goat Breeders Association

1.	Seven Hundred and Fifty-Six Miles by Google Maps	1
2.	'The Hills is Lonely'	5
3.	Cad and The Western Isles	13
4.	Heading to Princetown	25
5.	First Goats	37
6.	Goats in Lust	40
7.	Just Kidding	46
8.	Show Ring Debut	54
9.	The New Miss Peckwitt	65
10.	I Had Goats Once	72
11.	Wobbly New Beginnings	77
12.	Milton Abbot	86
13.	As Addictions Go, There Is No Better	95
14.	British Alpines and English Goats	107
15.	Ippy, The English Goat	110
16.	Robienne Cador	115
17.	Island Envy and Runrig	119
18.	All Falls Apart Again	122
19.	Heading North	134
20.	The Alternative Plan	144
21.	Tanglewood Times	149
22.	Edwardian Farm Fame	155
23.	All Good Things	158
24.	Artificial Insemination	166
25.	Doesn't Get Much Worse Than This	170
26.	2019 Moving On	180
27.	First Day Away	187
28.	Lost and Hopeless	191

29. 'From the Land Comes the Cloth'	201
30. Meeting The Kids	207
31. Coffee, Chips and Harris Tweed	215
32. The Mists Clear	221

Acknowledgments

About The Author

Foreword

The keeping of goats is what brought me into Viv's world. English goats in particular. There still are not many of them about and for those of us who are lucky enough to have them there is a common bond, an understanding if you like, a secret that we share between us.

The Meanderings of a Serial Goat Keeper is partly about Viv's goat keeping experiences – and trust me, those stories she tells about her goats are very real – but it is about far more than just goats. For instance, how life is changed on a moment of indiscretion, or unfounded trust in someone you do not really know. How family is so important. Forgiveness, honesty in one's own frailty, and, throughout the book, a strength of character that I suspect Viv does not even recognize as her own.

Yet Viv had seemed hesitant when she first mentioned that she was writing a book. As it was about one of her English goats, (who happened to be an ancestor of one of mine), it was with much persuasion that I encouraged her to send me those first chapters so that I could give some "honest feedback". Her skill at story telling was clear from the start and my husband could not hold a conversation with me until I had reached the end. It was only a rough draft, but the essence was there, and I finished reading those early chapters desperate to know what happened in the end –

so poor Viv was compelled to finish it, even if it was just for my satisfaction!

Looking back in time from late middle age, many of us can recognize the journey Viv has been on in her own life. The low self-expectation for women on leaving school (thanks to poor quality teaching at the time) which has then taken a lifetime of practical experience to teach us that we are indeed bright, can offer the world something more than, motherhood/secretarial skills/teaching/nursing. But ultimately, what is more important than parenting, in all honesty?

My memories of the locations Viv has described so well – Devon, Cornwall, Dartmoor, and Morwellham Quay in particular, date from the 1970's – a few years before Viv discovered them. However, her descriptions chime well with my personal memories and make me long for those heady times of youthful experiences with the Tamar Valley as my backdrop. I want to go back as strongly as Viv wants to go to the Western Isles… we all have unresolved dreams in us somewhere. I hope you enjoy reading this book as much as I have!

Johanna Seymour Tavernor

Secretary for the English Goat Breeders Association

Seven Hundred & Fifty-Six Miles

1. Seven Hundred & Fifty-Six Miles by Google Maps

'Got relatives on the islands, have you?'

'Oh! No, a goat, a billy goat.' I replied, startled at being spoken to and returning my boarding pass to the safety of a zipped pocket as I spoke. I smiled happily at the tweedy woman shaking a crumpled bag of mint imperials at me.

'Thank you,' I said taking one, delighted at the friendly gesture, although her expression struggled with itself at my explanation. Her eyes darted right and left, and her tongue moistened lips anxiously; I think the bag of mints would have been withdrawn if my hand wasn't already stuffed inside it.

I should have said friends, I thought. She took a breath.

'Really? That's… nice. My cousin's-mother's-aunt had a goat once. They eat anything, don't they? Oh, I've just remembered…' she bent to rifle through her suitcase. Whatever she was looking for was proving elusive, and the gap between us and the people in front was getting wider. I hovered awkwardly, unsure if I should continue to hover or carry on.

'Shall I ..?'

'No-no, you carry on. I…' she continued, bending to her task with an airy wave of the hand and inaudible to me now as I could no longer see her face. Assuming that I was dismissed, I left her rummaging and joined the tide of people that parted around her and now carried me towards what looked like a toy plane shimmering in the afternoon Edinburgh sunshine.

Well, I smiled to myself, *you asked for that*. A couple of decades being around goats should have taught me to think before I speak, especially when it comes to admitting to my goat habit. Friends often regretted their polite enquiry about what I was up to when I launched into my latest breeding plans, show ring hopes and fears for the next decade or so, and the individual yields and health status of every goat in my shed. Strangers often seemed to think I might be in league with the devil; from her reaction, I suspected the tweedy lady was one of the latter.

You've been out of it too long, I thought ruefully. It was five years since goats had been such a big part of my life. Perhaps that's what had caused my lapse, or perhaps I was just plain tired. I'd left my bed at two o'clock that morning, having barely slept since my head touched the pillow the night before. A complicated tangle of excitement and anxiety had kept me awake. I'd waited so long for this adventure, but I was nervous about tackling it on my own. My self-confidence had taken itself off somewhere else, and being solitary was a new experience.

I'd been discouraged from venturing out alone because as a child, a man had assaulted me in the woods around the lake where my family sailed. As I got older, I'd had a good supply of friends and then boyfriends to accompany me if I went out, and more recently I had rarely escaped the house without at least one of my six children - often joined by some of their friends too. I normally had the safety of the car for wherever I was going, occasionally I would take the train, but the only time I had ever flown was on a college jolly to the Paris Agricultural Show when I was seventeen. Hence the

Seven Hundred & Fifty-Six Miles

jitters at setting off on a journey that involved a long car drive in the early hours, plus two plane rides with their scary accompanying airports… and all completely unchaperoned. But, despite the collywobbles, I had managed thus far unscathed.

There had been an anxious moment when, having followed the arrows around the vastness of Bristol Airport car park to find my allocated space in only one circumnavigation, I remembered that it was impossible to lock my car without clambering out of the boot. But I reasoned no one was likely to steal my old car when there were far better models on offer, and there was nothing of value in it; they were welcome to the radio, as it didn't work anyway. So, left unlocked it was. And, despite my severe hearing loss in both ears, I was proud to have navigated the bewildering directions of officialdom and had managed to queue in all the right places inside the airport, without upsetting anyone or getting lost.

Now, here I was, about to embark on the last leg of my adventure. Before the day was done, I would have landed at my destination. Butterflies, or was it midges, were dancing highland flings in my tummy at the thought. I was headed for Stornoway Airport on Lewis, one of an archipelago of islands collectively known as The Outer Hebrides, The Western Isles, or Na h-Eileanan Siar if you have the Gaelic. Seven hundred and fifty-six miles as the crow would fly if it were following Google Maps and had nothing better to do that day. I just could not wait. This journey had been a long time coming; maybe I could tell my story to the tweedy lady if I ever saw her again. Despite my trepidation, midges, and barely contained excitement, I was as happy as a nanny goat in a feed shed as I boarded my flight.

4
Meanderings of a Serial Goat Keeper

I popped tweedy lady's mint into my mouth, de-stickying my hand on one of the complimentary lemony wipes and settled back into my seat as we waited for take-off. The cheerful cabin crew, in their smart red and black tartan, welcomed us with a dialect as gentle as a lullaby. I loved the lilting cadence of it so much that I felt moved to send a text to my eldest daughter, Abby, enthusing about everything Scottish, before turning off my phone for the flight.

We taxied to the start of the runway, lights like a million candles illuminating each side. There was a moment of calm before the exhilarating acceleration that took the wheels off the runway, making me think of Wilbur the albatross in Disney's *The Rescuers Down Under*, flapping inelegantly along for take-off with a sardine can strapped to his back.

I sucked harder on the mint as my ears popped, now trying to stifle a grin, as by then the cabin crew were exhorting us not to inflate life jackets inside the plane before ditching into the sea. My brain cell, freed from its earlier more stressful duties, amused itself by conjuring up a cartoon-like vision of ballon-like passengers bouncing off each other in a futile attempt to reach the exit and drop to the life raft below. Then, tired of those juvenile distractions, it turned its attention to the tattered paperback in my suitcase. The book that had begun my infatuation with the Western Isles, and the reason this journey was not just about visiting a billy goat.

2. 'The Hills is Lonely'

The book had been a chance purchase, one dismal day in 1971. The day is fixed in time by a photograph taken at The Kyle of Lochalsh. It's an unremarkable image, one of many crammed into a carrier bag full of others that never made the album. Where, from a wall in front of an expanse of dull-grey water, a monochrome fifteen-year-old me glowers at the lens, captured by my fathers old Kodak. In the distance is a darker mass of land, almost lost where Dads home developing skills left a little to be desired.

On the reverse of the photograph, however, my neat schoolgirl handwriting notes, *Isles of Skye in the background*, followed by an excited exclamation mark in heavy blue Biro. That one punctuation stroke with accompanying exultant dot summing up the awe of my first glimpse of the Hebrides. I had only ever heard 'Hebrides' applied to an expression meaning somewhere unimaginably nowhere up until then, so to find that not only was it a real place but was comparatively close to home was a revelation. That faded photo marks a beginning: not just the day I bought the book, but also the day I fell in love with an island.

I bought the book later that same afternoon. We were looking for a café, killing time before towing the hired caravan on to the next stop for the night. As I scuffed along behind my parents, a large poster in a gift shop window caught my eye. It advertised work by a local author and promised hilarious tales of crofting life on the Hebrides, and still in the grip of my earlier enlightenment about those islands, I called out for them to stop and suggested we might investigate. My mother's attention was immediately taken by some knitting kits for a traditional Shetland jumper. Although it was a complicated Fair Isle design she was an experienced knitter and it was well within her capabilities, perfect for the long evenings in the caravan, but Dad was clearly out of touch with the cost of wool and was taking some convincing. I left them working out whether buying all the components separately would be a cheaper option and made my way to the back of the shop, where I had spotted an echo of the poster I'd seen in the window. Maths had never been my forte anyway.

If I was honest, I was not really enjoying the holiday so far. I'd forgotten how much I disliked car travel, stuck in the back with the dog while the motion and Dad chain-smoking made me feel sick. Plus, the evenings, in the confined space of the touring van made for an unwieldy threesome. My father was off work having had some sort of breakdown, and I was under orders not to upset him. The holiday was supposed to be helping his recuperation, but I didn't understand what he was going through as nothing much was discussed with me. I was trying hard to be a model daughter but didn't seem to be making a very good job of it. I just hoped that my *nose stuck in a book*, a comment often used to imply that I should be doing something else, might divert attention from what exam options I was going to choose. That, and the wagging finger that accompanied the inevitable lectures about '…the world not owing me a living.'

'The Hills is Lonely'

The truth was that I had no idea what I wanted to do. Everything had started to slither downhill when I was moved to a new school. Bath Art School, my former school, had closed, a victim of the new comprehensive system. I mourned for the creative, relaxed atmosphere I had left behind and missed the fatherly headteacher, Mr Hall. I found the regimentation and rule-by-fear of my new school restrictive and had already been unfairly branded a rebel because I dared to make a helpful suggestion. Constructive criticism had been encouraged at my old school as progressive thinking.

I found I was behind in some subjects. All lessons at the Art School were based around art, such as in Math's, we designed and coloured in tessellating shapes and stuck them on the back wall. So, I was completely at a loss at my new school, where my classmates had been using log tables since the first year. I never really caught up.

We'd had career talks, of course, but none of the conventional jobs for girls at that time appealed. I couldn't see myself as a secretary, or a nurse, or a policewoman. I had nurtured a shy, almost guilty, hope of being a writer. Something that had been encouraged at the Art school, but cruelly squashed by my new English teacher. Instead of guidance towards the Booker Prize, my angsty, epic prose was handed back covered in red pen along with a concerned 'chat' about considering professional help for my problems. Mortified and ashamed, I vowed never to write again, but that decision left me with no alternative career plan. I needed a direction, something to make me feel that life was worth the gargantuan effort it appeared to require. So far, escaping the world by way of a good book was the best I had come up with.

Meanderings of a Serial Goat Keeper

I worked my way through the knots of people exclaiming over tartan mugs and purses shaped like sporrans until I found myself in front of the book stand; Lillian Beckwith was the featured author. *The Hills is Lonely* was the first of the series, with a hand-painted cover-image of a little fishing boat chugging along a wild coastline backed by moorland hills. This was something different to what the school library had to offer and looked like it could be my kind of book. I read the title again with a thrill of delicious glee thinking that someone had made the most horrendous printing error and flipped it over to read the blurb:

'When Lillian Beckwith advertised for a quiet place in which to rest, she received the following answer from the Hebrides:

Dear Madam
Its just now I saw your advert when I got the book for the knitting pattern I wanted from my cousin Catriona. I am sorry I did not write sooner if you are fixed up if you are not fixed up I have a good good stone house and tiles and my brother Ruari who will wash down with lime twice every year. Ruari is married and lives close by. She is not damp. I live by myself and you could have the room that is not the kitchen and a bedroom reasonable. I was in the kitchen of the lairds house till lately when he was changed God rest his soul the poor old gentleman that he was. You would be very welcomed. I have a cow also for milk and eggs and the minister at the manse will be referee if you wish such.
Yours affectionately
Morag McDugan

'The Hills is Lonely'

P.S. She is not thatched.

THE HILLS IS LONELY is the enchanting story of the extremely unusual 'rest cure' which followed.'

The dual-purpose cow for milk and eggs made me laugh and I finally twigged that the title 'error' was intentional, a refreshing break from writing convention that impressed me no end. The book was quickly paid for and stowed away in the pocket of my orange Helly Hansen, where it called to me for the rest of the afternoon. I couldn't wait to stick my nose in it.

That night Mum cast on the rib of her new jumper. Soft fawn wool from the first of not just one, but two kits purchased that afternoon. I was to be the lucky recipient of the second one. Dad must have been in a good mood! He, meanwhile, tut-tutted from the depths of his Telegraph about something called Watergate, leaving me alone to devour my find to the gentle hiss and pop of the gas lamps that cast mellow shadows and smelt of camping. Lillian's portrayal of a simple Hebridean life with her charming landlady, baking scones on a griddle before wandering off to milk the cow, were vividly real to me and spoke in a way nothing else ever had. This was my answer. This was the life I wanted. I just had to work out how.

After that holiday, a chat with a patient, enlightened, new career teacher put forward the idea that a year at Lackham College might be for me. He had found a course in General Agriculture (for women) with Rural Home Economics, that would combine my love of animals with the practical school subjects in which I had done reasonably well. More importantly, known affectionately as the 'farmer's wife' course because it covered everything a diligent farmers wife should know, from rearing chicks and milking, to making wine and cheese, it struck me as ideal for someone who wanted to live on a remote island croft.

I was just in time. With the voice of feminism shouting ever louder, the gender-specific nature of the course was condemned as too sexist, and we were told that mine was the last year it would run. It was a perfect opportunity in so many ways and I added many useful skills to my increasing repertoire of crafts and self-sufficiency knowledge for my intended new life. Not so helpful to my plan, was the effect of the slim ratio of girls to strapping lads, which led to the inevitable pairing-off of us girls, and my dream being toppled from first place on my list of priorities.

Mike was one of three asking me out at the time. We had met when he was being a hero. Walking along in a gaggle as usual on our way back from from Vet lectures one dark evening, some of the lads had ambushed us girls, manhandled us into their cars and then dumped us a few miles away from college to walk back. This was to teach us a lesson for tying their cars together. Mike was one of the good guys, who had got wind of what was going on and had set out to rescue us... all the girls love a hero don't they!

Word about Mike's interest had reached my ear via his mate Bob, but I was supposed to be in a long-distance relationship with a guy I had met while Youth Hostelling that summer with an Art School friend. So, later that week I knocked at his door intending to politely turn him down but was stopped in my tracks when the door opened... because he had bare feet. Their nakedness was slightly embarrassing somehow and the soft black hairs on his toes gave him an honest

'The Hills is Lonely'

vulnerability. The reason for their exposed state was because he had just had a shower, he explained. Could this mean that he cares about personal hygiene? I wondered. With the death knell of the holiday romance clanging somewhere in the distance, he found some socks and shoes, and together we set off for The George in Lacock.

His presence was powerful, emphasised by a sweeping full-length trench coat and a shock of thick dark hair, and his eyes were the palest blue I had ever seen. He was very much the gentleman too, opening doors and pulling out my chair for me to sit down. In short, if I overlooked the mutton chop sideburns, he was the most handsome chap I had ever been out with, and quite definitely a man, after all the boys I'd been involved with before. It felt fabulous to be treated like a woman, and not one of the lads for a change. The clincher was that at over six foot, he was taller than me. This was a rare occurrence, and one worth hanging onto as I was five-foot-eleven-and-a-little-bit myself, with ambitions of being able to lay my head on a man's chest as we smooched. But while that particular fantasy was still not quite fulfilled without getting a crick in my neck, at least he wasn't at eye level to my boobs. A girl has to be thankful for small mercies.

It was November the 21st 1973. A date that may still be written on a Phil Collins album somewhere in a vintage record collection. Sorrowfully the Hebridean plan shuffled off to the back burner to sulk, displaced by this new dish that was cooking, but it was never quite forgotten. Lillian's books followed me to every place I called home and kept the pot stirring.

Which is why, I told myself (possibly out loud) while trying not to annoy the man next to me as I experimented with the planes' armrests, that although thirty-odd years had passed since that dreary caravan holiday with my parents, this long-awaited expedition to the land of my youthful ambitions, at such a crossroads in my life, was meant to be. And all because of a completely out-of-the-blue phone call.

3. Cad and the Western Isles

A few weeks earlier, the insistent 'perrrp perrrp' of the phone had disturbed my washing up.

'Who's that then?' I asked Flynn-the-dog, drying my hands on my jeans as I stepped over him to reach for the phone. He flump-flumped his tail in reply, fanning tumbleweeds of fluff to the skirtings. A man's voice answered my greeting.

'It's Roland here'.

'Roland?' I screwed up my eyes trying to think. Was that the name of the solicitor dealing with Mum's estate? I hoped it was. I needed that particular ordeal to be over. Mum's death had hit me hard at a time when everything else seemed to be falling apart too. Some good news was much needed. I shut my eyes to hear better and swapped ears, feeling like Eeyore when he asked Piglet to say it again on the other side. Intuition told me this was important. I told him that my hearing was a bit duff and asked if he would repeat, and could he please slow down a bit.

'It's Roland speaking. We have Cad here. CAD, C-A-D,' he shouted down the phone enunciating each word with exaggerated care.

'We wondered if you'd like to come and see him? He's had a busy time... Twenty-seven nannies visited this spring alone, but practically all the goats on the island are related to him now... his feet are playing him up... So, we're giving him one last luxury summer. We'd love you to be here for it.'

I wasn't keeping up, but it clearly wasn't Mum's solicitor, that much I had worked out. My brain was rummaging quickly through cached files to try and come up with something else. I didn't understand. My goats all had to go when I'd left Milton Abbot. What was he talking about? Then I twigged; by Cad, he meant, Cador, a male English goat I'd bred years ago, but I was still puzzled. Island? What island? I'd thought Cad was with Janet in Portsmouth… which, when I last looked, may have been near the sea but was quite definitely not an island. He tried again.

'We're on the Isle of Lewis. You know, the Outer Hebrides, Scotland.'

The land of Lillian Beckwith and they were inviting me to go there! My legs felt wobbly and I sat down heavily onto the bottom stair. I heard myself murmuring polite platitudes such as 'I couldn't possibly...' and 'too good of you..' before agreeing that I would look up the plane times and let them know by the end of the day.

'Well, my day has certainly changed.' I told the dog, who sent a bit more fluff rolling over the floor. I headed for the kettle in a daze. Earlier, I'd been depressed, grey from so much that had happened over the last few years, but now colours were popping around me like fireworks. Being invited to spend ten days on the very islands I had dreamed of all these years had to be more than a coincidence. Who knows what opportunities might lie ahead? I could not wait to get on that plane.

My new friends had promised to pick me up from the airport at Stornoway, Lewis. I wondered how they would know me and joked about wearing a red carnation or carrying a copy of the Goating Times, but they assured me there was no need. I was flattered, thinking that my fame must have gone before me, but to be honest they were right. I must have stuck out like

Cad and the Western Isles

a goat in a field of sheep, as I made my way carefully down the rickety steps from the plane. Of the dozen or so people hurrying past me, I am sure I was the only one glassy-eyed, lost and more than a little spaced out from all the travelling. It had been a long day.

I looked around the terminal building, which was bigger than I'd expected for a remote island. Its cool hues of blue and grey were welcome after the glare outside. Around the walls were toothpaste-fresh images of foaming waves smashing into rocky headlands, juxtaposed with endless white beaches kissed by water so startlingly blue, that I assumed they had been exaggerated by an over-enthusiastic publicity team. My eyes continued their sweep of the room, then doubled back to a couple waiting by the potted plastic palms at the exit.

Their eyes met mine. It could not have been anyone but my hosts. There is something unquantifiable but instantly recognisable between goat keepers.

I was still a bit awestruck as they stowed my bag into the boot of their car and me onto the back seat, before setting off on the thirty-odd-mile journey to their home. My first impression was that the land around Stornoway seemed flat and lacked character. There was also rusting industrial rubbish languishing on edges of crofts, which wasn't the image of the Hebrides that I'd held in my heart all this time. Fly-tipping is such a taboo where I live in the South West, that it surprised me to see it scarring the landscape here in such a beautiful place. Roland explained that getting rid of scrap is expensive and difficult when you live on an island, adding somewhat defensively, that it is still very much a working environment. I supposed, trying to put a positive spin on it, that in a landscape of few trees, these decaying old vehicles made good habitats for nesting birds or field mice.

I was, however, impressed by the roads which seemed well maintained with an enviable absence of the potholes I was used to in Devon. The road we were following was the main artery down through the island, mostly single track with freshly painted white lines tracing the sides. Such clear borders must make it a lot less likely for drivers to wander over the edge by mistake, I thought, especially in the mist. They looked quite authoritative too. A better way of saying keep off the grass than any signage. A simple deterrent to keep picnickers from pulling off the road and spoiling what little grazing there was. There were no excuses for chewing up the verges to allow cars to go by either, as there were plentiful designated passing places. Every single one was labelled with a diamond-shaped notice announcing that it was a Passing Place, in case you didn't realise. They are not, Roland emphasised sternly, lay-bys for stopping to admire the view.

We passed a small plantation of trees, a rarity here. Apparently, there is evidence of large forests following on after the Ice Age, but the trees had dwindled over time. Changing climate may be one reason, but legend has it that marauding Vikings purposely destroyed the trees to prevent the islanders from building boats and defending themselves. Then there were the clearances when the land was taken for grazing sheep. The few trees we did pass were skeletal, their lifeless branches reaching in a forlorn prayer to the sky; 'acid rain,' Roland informed me.

But then, after negotiating a sharpish bend with a meander where hopeful Blackface sheep lingered by a

Cad and the Western Isles

roadside hayrack, I had my first sight of one of the many inland lochs. My new tour guide, noticing the drop of my jaw, obligingly pulled into a passing place to let me admire the view. To a backdrop of tartan hills, topped by a summer sky that was stuffed with billowing cumulus making their languid way northeast, the waters of the lochan looked stunningly beautiful. The glassy surface ruffled from time to time with a hint of a cats-paw as the breeze caressed it, and there were mallards just being ducks on a lazy day. If proof was needed that the vivid blues of the airport images had not been photo-shopped, then this was it. I could feel tears prickling and emotion stole my voice. I was an exhausted wreck from struggling to stay strong for too long, at a time when I was all out of giving. Functioning but not there, uncertain of the future and sometimes afraid. Yet here I was, and all because of Cad. It was too much to take in, and something inside me gave way. The bunched-up feelings I'd been managing to suppress threatened to spill. This was a place where the winds could carry the hurt and bewilderment away, and the moors and the lochs could heal me. Embarrassed at the threatening tears, I got back in the car and we trundled on.

Debbie and Roland's home was a traditionally built one-and-a-half storey croft house. It was effectively a bungalow, with a roof low enough that gales would pass over, but with room enough inside to squeeze in an upstairs bedroom - if you were careful with your head.

The front door took us through a ground floor bedroom into the kitchen, where a solid fuel stove was making the room unbearably hot. Behind a cheery red-and-white check curtain was the bathroom and loo;

'best to whistle when you're in there,' I was advised. Next to that were the sitting room and the stairs to the upper floor. It was more of a ladder if I'm honest. Steep narrow treads reared up to a hole in the ceiling, which served as the entrance to what was to be my bedroom for the duration of my stay. Once ensconced, it was cosy up there under the eaves. A comfy-looking double bed occupied most of one end of the room, with the inverted V of the roof arching over it. Jewelled rows of homemade wine marched in disarray across the room at the other end. Although fresh fruit and veg are not plentiful on the islands, my hosts had an arrangement with a wholesaler in Stornoway, picking up greengrocer waste once a week. Some of it never made it as far as the goats feed buckets; I can particularly recommend the Banana, Vintage 2003.

By the time I came down, the kettle was singing and meal preparation underway. Next to the butler sink where Debbie was washing lettuce, was the back entrance. The top half of the stable door had been opened and several goats from the yard immediately outside were scrabbling for treats. I was handed a packet of ginger biscuits to dish out and was introduced to each in turn. I was pleased to see them, I missed my goats, but the one I really wanted to see was clearly above such youthful shenanigans. I looked for him beyond the bobbing heads and there he was, Robienne Cador, named after a legendary Duke of Cornwall, a relative of King Arthur. Cad had left my small herd of minority breed, English goats as a kid, and now he was all grown up. His soft grey baby coat had long gone, replaced with longer coarser hair that formed a full beard and mane around his head. The characteristic black cross of the English breed traced his spine, followed on down over his shoulders and fanned out in a thick dark stripe that spread across his chest and down his legs. He looked magnificent. His bottom jaw circled as he chewed the cud, sunbathing with his head turned towards us in mild curiosity but too lazy to move. I was so proud of him. He looked relaxed and so confident of his regal status, that the male kid challenging him didn't bother him at all. He sneezed at the dust kicked up by the Plymouth Black Rock hens and shook his head at them in mild threat.

I spoke his name softly and he looked over. Did he remember me?

I had once been his 'mum', bottle rearing him with four other kids born that year at Milton Abbot. During the day they would go out onto the side garden, where I could see them while I was washing up. They had rocks to jump off and the duck-house roof to climb on, teetering on tippy-toed hind legs to reach the fronds of ivy that hung so temptingly from the wall separating us from the vicarage next door. Elsie, my youngest daughter, about three years old at the time, loved to play with them and laughed in delight as she ran up and down while they jumped and skipped with her. When they were tired of that, she would lead them around the garden on bits of old baler twine, practising her showmanship, copying me in a way that made my heart melt. It was a partnership of such trust between young things. I mentioned this to Roland.

'Ah that would explain why he was such a hit with the Brownies!' he said fondly. 'We had the local pack here to see the goats one evening. He was so patient; put up with them brushing and combing him for hours. They adored him too. We had to print off photos of him for them all. He's on the walls of a lot of little girl's bedrooms. I wondered if he had been around children before.'

Cad was a minority breed English goat, so scarce that I hadn't known about them until quite late on in my goat-keeping life as they were not a breed 'recognised' by the British Goat Society (the umbrella organisation for all the affiliated goat societies and clubs in the U.K.). So, there was no mention of them in any of my books. They were becoming increasingly popular, especially with smallholders, because of their thrifty, hardy, nature, but there were still not many about.

Roland obviously had a soft heart when it came to animals, but I suspected that there were some human things he had issues with, such as new-fangled mobile phones. Mobiles were simple affairs in 2004. They could be persuaded to make calls or send laborious abbreviated text, if lucky enough to be within signal, which came in rare pockets. A signal had made itself known on our drive from the airport, causing the phone in my pocket to vibrate loudly and telling me that a heap of texts had just hit the mailbox. I'd gone to take it out of my pocket, but something about Roland's eyebrows reflected in his rear-view mirror made me hesitate. I didn't want to be impolite so,I decided that news from home could wait. However, I regretted this later as there was no signal at the house. I was worried that I might have to wait for several days until we happened back to that one spot again; but after tea, Debbie took me on a tour of their land and indicated that if I climbed the heap of rocks adjacent to the right-hand side of the house, there was sometimes a signal there... if the wind was in the right direction, there was a full moon, and ideally, if it happened to be a leap

Cad and the Western Isles

year... I clambered up eagerly. I was desperate to share the news of a visitor expected later that evening.

Our forthcoming visitor had grown up on a neighbouring croft. In days of yore, the tenant crofters just built another house on the open moor when one was needed, gathering local stone for the structure and making use of the plentiful supply of peat as a roof covering. The animals, when not occupying one end of the house, wandered at will, not needing fences as they had learned where they lived from their mothers. Something handed down by generations of animals, called 'hefting' on Dartmoor. I'm sure there is a Gaelic equivalent.

In our compartmented lives on the mainland today, where we fight over parking spaces, this sort of freedom is a hard concept to imagine. But it continued for hundreds of years until it was decided by the higher eschelons that sheep made a better profit than people. The land was enclosed, and parcels allocated to the tenants with the grazing on a rotational system (known as run-rig). This was carried out by a middleman, or Tackman, acting for the owner of the islands. Because of the new system, many of the children then grew up to be landless. Some emigrated, others were forced to leave to seek work on the mainland. Some quietly flouted the new regulations and built new houses within their family's allotment of land, sharing what resources they could. This explanation is an oversimplified Sassenach interpretation of the systematic depopulation of the islands and does no justice to what many families must have suffered.

Meanderings of a Serial Goat Keeper

My friend's house, I believe to be one such addition. It was also mid-way between one settlement and the next, and so made the perfect place to meet for the traditional Ceilidhs. These could be lively affairs with dancing, or just a chance to catch up on the gossip and enjoy- a good story. Most villages had a storyteller, a tradition passed down from generation to generation of the same family. I knew of this from a favourite childhood book, *Seal Morning*, written by Rowena Farre, published in 1957. She explains that those blessed with the gift of the stories were also likely to be healers, fortune-tellers, and to have second sight. Love potions could be bought, and herbs and spells used to heal the sick. They also strongly believed in ghosts, banshees, evil spirits... and faeries. Hence my excitement, because that very evening we were expecting a visit from Kenny Macleod. Kenny, Roland explained, was a descendant of the traditional storytellers for the area, and although he now lived on the mainland, he had not lost the gift. Adding, with a furtive glance around to check that no one was listening, that Kenny was *King of the Faeries*.

I didn't believe in faeries, of course I didn't – did I?, Yet remembering the warnings in *Seal Morning*, and knowing of the dire consequences of upsetting the little folk, from West Country folklore, there is always that element of doubt. Being a broad and open minded sort of person who respects other peoples beliefs, I said nothing, just nodded sagely. Inside, I was bubbling and couldn't wait to tell the family back home of such an important visitor. *King of the Faeries*. They would be so impressed!

Cad and the Western Isles

Kenny told of water horses that whisked beautiful young girls to bottomless lochs, of enchanted seals that turned into people who sang mournful songs on the shores, and of spirits disguised as animals. His appearance might have been disappointingly conventional, but his voice swayed and whispered like grasses ripe for mowing. His voice was so hypnotic, that my eyelids refused to stay open and, I'm mortified to admit, that I nodded off. I was horrified at my bad manners when I had been so honoured and was worried that I might have offended... and what the consequences might be... but Kenny reassured me that it often happened and he was not surprised as, after all, some of the stories were indeed for soothing fretful bairns to sleep.

The other stories, those of monsters and vengeful spirits, also had a purpose. With their parents so hard working, children often had to walk several miles unaccompanied over boggy croft land with few roads, pocked with dangerous inland lochs and certainly no streetlamps. Believing that countless horrors were waiting out there for anyone who strayed could keep them safe. He admitted that the stories had terrified him as a child, and even now he would never step off the road after dark. Kenny was a remarkable man, and I admired him greatly. It seemed sad that such gifted man no longer lived on his homeland but I belive he had found happiness with his male partner. Something which may have been difficult amid the traditional attitudes still found on the island.

I'm embarrassed to say that as I lay in my cosy bed later that night, still in the aftermath of Kenny's tales, I couldn't relax until I had checked out the shadows cast by the dimpsy light. But it wasn't just ghostly corners that were keeping me awake; tomorrow, we were going to see a Tweed shop in Harris that was for sale. I hoped it was serendipity, the chance I was looking for, but then again… what if it was? Abby's anxious reply to my excited text sent from the plane settled resolutely somewhere between my ambition and my conscience.

'You will come home Mum, won't you?'

4. Heading to Princetown

The Unitied Kingdom has around forty pockets of feral goats. Not strictly wild, some are descended from escapees or goats abandoned, others deliberately introduced for conservation purposes These hardy, little hairy goats resemble most peoples image of what goats look like. Their undeserved, reputation of eating anything and butting you if you were silly enough to bend over in their presence, garnered mostly from childrens story books. As that was also my childhood image of a goat, it was with some trepidation that I followed my school friend Sally down the path between the vegitables to take Joan some peelings. Joan was her Mum's goat and nothing like what I was expecting. She was much bigger for a start, with a short, sleek, shiny black and white coat, enchanting rather than fierce. I fell head over heels instantly. Not only was she the most beautiful animal I had ever seen, but she also produced the milk we always had when I came to visit, so useful too. I had never noticed any difference from the cows' milk I was used to, so it was not the vile spew of witches that popular opinion had made it out to be. I was impressed. Meeting Joan was a turning point in my life and from then on, I wanted one. But, from meeting Joan to having some goats myself was to take a further ten years or so.

After agricultural college, and by then engaged to Mike of the hairy toes, I worked as a Receptionist and Veterinary Nurse at a large veterinary practice of seven partners in Chippenham. Where, for four pounds a week, I was able to live in the flat above the surgery. I wasn't so keen on the reception work, or the accounts, but loved mixing up the medicines and the animal side of things, especially helping with the operations. The other animal nurse employed had been a nurse of the human variety, but I had no formal training apart from the Vet Lectures at Lackham, and they were more about cows and sheep than dogs and cats.

After two years, during one of the many times when I had lost patience with the charming but untrammelled Mike and had finished with him, I asked if I could train to qualify as a RANA (Royal Animal Nursing Auxiliary). At that time, it required two years of working at a practice, which I had done, but also one of the Vets to mentor me for a year. One of the small animal vets I assisted was persuaded to plead my case to the other six partners, who were not keen. But Chris convinced them that I could do it and that he would personally supervise and coach me until the two years at Bristol Veterinary College took over. This was an extraordinary opportunity and I was really excited by it.

But then, weakened by the regular roses, beseeching letters, and because my legs almost gave way when I saw him with someone else in Bath one day, I pushed aside my misgivings. With Mike back in my life, we set a wedding date, despite the many objections raised by his parents.

With my head full of wedding plans, there seemed little point carrying on with my vet nursing aspirations. I believed that being a wife and mother was a full-time job and, at that time, it was still possible for a man to earn a 'living wage' to support his family. So, I did as my mother had done before me, and gave up the chance of a career to be a wife. In doing so, I let my veterinary champion down badly. I knew he was disappointed in me, and it was not the same working there after that. More crucially for me and the rest of my life, I had chucked away my best chance to be financially independent. And just to make certain that his Roman Catholic parents thought the absolute worst of me, I was twelve weeks pregnant by the time of the wedding ceremony.

The drought of the 1976 summer broke the night before our wedding day, and it continued to thunder all through the service. Perhaps, I should have taken note of that bad omen.

Instead of a career for myself, I threw myself into supporting my husband in his. I trotted after him, like a good little wifey, all over the country, washing his socks while he racked up debts training as an Engineer and collecting letters after his name. Then, he tried one job after another until, having got himself the sack from his latest job (of selling finance to farmers), he gleefully announced that he was off to Beaconsfield to be an officer cadet. He appeared to have no apparent thought for me, or our girls, Abby and Tam, or our third baby that I was carrying by then.

I hoped it was another of his fads, like the sheep farming in the Falklands idea, but as the weeks went on it was clear that not only was he was determined to go, but he was looking forward to it. I know millions of forces women go through this all the time, but I came from a culture where men bring their cherished women a cup of tea in bed in the morning and was so hurt that he could up and leave us so easily that I wondered if he would even miss us. I didn't know how I was going to live without him. This was not what I had signed up for, or how it happened in books.

The Health Visitor was also concerned that three children under five might be too much for a breastfeeding mum on her own, especially as Robin was barely two weeks old when Mike left us. She arranged for extra help for me, but I was appalled at this idea, taking her gesture as a slight. I didn't want anyone to think I couldn't cope, and worried that she had alerted social services to look out for signs of neglect or abuse in the children. It felt as though I had fallen from being a respected and capable mum to the sort of person you might read about in the papers.

Well, no one was going to find fault with my children, or the way I looked after them. If Mary Lamont, an ancestor from whom I take my middle name, could survive the battle of Dunoon with her three sons when her husband and two hundred of her clan were slaughtered by the Campbells, then I could probably cope with my three in the leafy suburbs of Warwickshire. I rallied and found a determination dormant until then. Nothing was left to do later, even buttons got sewn back on the minute I discovered a shirt or blouse that was missing one, and cups and plates were washed as we used them. I made sure there was nothing for 'Busy Lizzie's' duster to do on her twice-weekly visits. Instead, we sat and had a cup of tea and a natter. Once I got off my high horse, I discovered that she was great company and more than happy to sit and cuddle Robin while I had a nap. So, I grew to look forward to her coming and the few minutes respite she gave me.

Heading to Princetown

However, as the weeks went on, the punishing, self-imposed regime that I had set myself began to have a negative effect. I started to resent my husband coming home for his occasional visits, disrupting our routine and seemingly, just to get his leg over. He didn't appear to notice that the restrictive diet to lose my baby belly had shifted a few more pounds, or my efforts to look nice for him, or that everything was in order. His sprawl of belongings dumped in the hallway irritated me, and the way he yelled at the kids upset me. What right did he have to do that? The pat on the back, that I was too proud to ask for, never happened and his brief appearances were unsettling for all of us. The children took ages to calm down after he left us for his mates again, adding to my stress levels. I was overwhelmed and depressed.

One afternoon in September my parents, on their way to their cruiser moored nearby on the Warwickshire canal, found me distressed and sweating on the bed with a teasy baby who couldn't feed, and pestered by two fretful girls who wanted my attention. Mum took Robin off me and shooed the others away for their tea. Dad marched me off to the Doctors, then the chemists to collect antibiotics for a raging breast abscess, purchasing bottles and milk formula to get Robin off the breast.

Having sorted the immediate issues, Mum and Dad continued on to their boating holiday; leaving me wondering how I was going to rest as the doctor told me to, and unable to feed my baby, feeling like I had failed as both a mother, wife and daughter.

It was nearly Christmas when I finally snapped. I had been invited to Beaconsfield for the posh, end-of-term 'do' for the officer cadets. Mike picked me up from the station, a bundle of nerves after a lengthy journey, having navigated my way across London, all by myself... and it had started to snow.

On arrival, the duty phone call to Mum who was minding the children revealed that Tam was not well... again, and running a temperature. There was no question of me going straight home, as by this time the snow was heavy enough to have caused all further rail services to be cancelled. I knew Mum would manage, but my guilt at being so far away from my children when they needed me, and the helplessness of knowing there was nothing I could do, niggled all evening.

Neither was I impressed with the duty mingling of the senior officers' wives pressed into service for the evening. I might sound like a country bumpkin with my 'Wurzels' accent, but I did know how to hold a knife and fork from years of sailing club dinners, and I didn't appreciate being talked down to. Which was possibly why I was not as polite as I should have been when an especially snooty officer's wife laughed at my heated assurance that no child of mine would be packed off to boarding school, as she was suggesting.

'If my husband is posted abroad', I emphasised, 'he will be going on his own.' Having dismissed me as an unsuitable officer's wife, she moved on to find another victim to demoralise, leaving me wondering what I was doing there: It wasn't my world, and I didn't want it to be.

I tried to catch Mike's eye for rescue, but he was sat in a corner with his friends, his arm around the only girl on his course, obviously having a great time. A new bit of music started and one of his gang got up and started to strip to it. I clic-clacked over to Mike in my heels,

Heading to Princetown

but instead of the reassurance I so desperately needed, he suggested that it was time I went.

'The lads want to enjoy themselves,' he said, nodding toward the stripper. It was then, the only time in my life, that I completely, and very publicly, lost my rag.

The dynamics of our relationship changed after that. My respect for this man as protector and provider for his family was gone, replaced by the dangerous knowledge that I had survived, not only without him but despite him. Where I had looked to him for everything, he'd forced me to look to myself. I found that I had an iron box in my head where emotions could be locked away, enabling a numbness that helped me to carry on. Perhaps he realised something of that, or maybe it was the home truths that I'd spat at him that night, or maybe just the ten mile runs in full kit, but whatever it was he decided that army life was not for him after all. He bought himself out, escalating our debt, and come back home to us.

'We could try again, couldn't we?'

Selling the house in Evesham raised sufficient funds to keep the bailiffs from the door, leaving enough money for a small deposit on an old railway workers cottage in Devon. It was a 'fixer upper' but it looked solid enough in the photographs and was only a short run from Plymouth College of St Mark and St John, where Mike had now enrolled to do a three-year teaching degree.

Frustratingly I could have nothing to do with the arrangements, having to leave it to Mike to travel the hundred and sixty miles back and forth while I was stuck in the Midlands with the three children, but I was happy with Devon as a place to live because it was where my father's family had lived for generations. Mum's family came from Wiltshire, but they had moved to Plymouth when she was young. Devon, for me, offered family roots. My parents had met at Bertie Jackson's riding stable, in Roborough, and were married a few years later at the Church of Emmanuel, just outside Plymouth. My brother and I were christened at the same church by special dispensation, although our family lived in Bath by then. I also knew Devon well from the annual visits 'home' to see both sets of grandparents and an assortment of relatives. Devon had always been heralded as a special place, but with Mike at the helm of managing everything, I was forced to hope it would all work out.

Moving down proved to be a harrowing journey. Fortunately, the children and my dog were with Mum, so they were safe. Mike had gone on ahead in a flatbed lorry he had bought to move us. I was following in our brave little A30 van complete with a trailer load of assorted belongings, including my four Khaki Campbell ducks and Molly the kitten. We were heavily overloaded, making what little stopping power the ancient van did have mostly ineffective. As well as the foot brake, I had to use the handbrake and gears to slow me down, which was nerve wreaking as well as mentally exhausting, having to concentrate hard to anticipate the need to stop well in advance. I had only passed my test a few years before, and since then had rarely driven, as Mike always took the wheel when we went out and I hardly ever went anywhere without him. This was the longest drive I had ever done on my own.

The engine overheated on the dual carriageway and I was forced to pull into a handy lay-by. Where I sat

Heading to Princetown

enveloped in a cloud of steam wondering what to do. I knew enough not to try to unscrew the radiator cap until it had cooled, so decided that sitting tight was my best option. Fortuantely, Mike eventually noticed that I was no longer behind him and came back to rescue me. The remains of a bottle of water, warm from the sun did the trick and we set off again. A few miles further on, after turning off the A38 at Ashburton, and making our painful way up Holne Hill, I noticed that the lorry was having problems. I was getting closer and closer, until I could go no slower and had to stop. Unfortunately, the little van had nothing left to hold us on that steep gradient, and van, ducks, kitten, and I, slipped gracefully back down the road until the skewing of the trailer crashed us into a wall. Fortunately, no one was hurt, and unbelievably, no damage was done to the car or trailer.

Water for both vehicles was sourced from a nearby house, and off we set again. I knew we weren't far off now, but there was worse yet to come. The winding slope coming down towards The Warren pub was like a helter-skelter. Even in first gear, with the handbrake yanked on full, and the brake pedal flat to the floor, I still careered down at a terrifying speed with the engine screaming.

The kitten was meowing pitifully in her box and the ducks quacked their alarm in the trailer behind, but we made it to the bottom, breathed, and pressed on.

It was with massive relief that I pulled up in front of our new home in Princetown, shaken and wobbly, but thankful to be in one piece. I had a cautious look around; the sun was setting over the moor towards Plymouth in a blaze of reds and golds and the house looked solid, square and friendly. It was on the end of a terrace of four, and it boasted a large side garden bordered by a privet hedge with about an acre of rough ground to its right. Through my tears of relief at still being alive, I decided that it was my turn now. I may not be able to have goats in the Hebrides, but I could have some right here in the garden.

The ducks, bless their stout little hearts, never missed a beat. Four nice fresh eggs were waiting the next morning when I let them out for slug patrol.

I soon learned that Princetown was not for the fainthearted. At fourteen hundred feet above sea level, it spends much of its time hiding morosely under cloud. The swirling mists that gave Sir Arthur Conan Doyle inspiration for *The Hound of The Baskervilles* offered the occasional glimpse of a scattering of houses and shops, a couple of pubs, and the village school that the children attended. Dartmoor prison, built during the Napoleonic wars, sits like a scab on the browns, purples, and greens of the surrounding moors. It's hard to ignore its forbidding granite frown, that affects the atmosphere as if watching everything you do. It is a hard place, with fierce horizontal rain that stings faces. Knuckles, exposed from pushing buggies, need to be unclenched one finger at a time and toes itch with chilblains. The chilly Dartmoor winds whistled into our old house through every chink, and we kept a heat bulb on all the time in the loo to stop the pipes from freezing.

Initially, we only had two open fires to heat the house, but eventually were able to fit an old range, that a neighbour was throwing away. That gave us one warmish room at least, and we were able to keep it fed on waste wood from Mike's course. I worried that Robin would freeze in his cot as it was so cold that first

Heading to Princetown

winter. But for a few treasured days in the summer, a deep breath would fill your lungs with clean air and the montage of ponies, sheep, and cattle pulling at the tough grasses of the moor stood in sharp relief to the backdrop of budding shoots of coconut-smelling gorse. It wasn't quite as remote as the Western Isles, but I reckoned that the wilds of Dartmoor were a darn good compromise. I would make this work.

The poor old A30 van never recovered from that journey down and was eventually replaced by a Morris Traveller that I bought from the landlords of the Merrivale Inn on the moor. It was the Morris that took the children and me to see some goats that were for sale.

It had been a dry summer, and as I parked, clouds of dust raised from the farmyard and hung in the air. It tasted of childhood games in parched summer flower beds and caught in a throat already dry with excitement. I wasn't entirely sure what goats were for sale, as Mrs Turner had been a bit obscure on the phone. So, I'd not said much to the children about our mission in case it all fell through. I was sure David MacKenzie, who offered a lot of sound advice on buying a goat in his book *Goat Husbandry*, would not approve of this ill-researched approach, but finding any had proved tricky. In excited preparation I'd joined The Devon Goat Society, but whilst I learnt much about plaiting nifty goat leads from baler twine, I soon realised that decent goats were hard to come by. Goats had become popular following the recent publication of John Seymour's book, *Self Sufficiency*, thereby contributing to the scarcity of the sort of goat of which MacKenzie might approve. Buying a scrubby non-pedigree goat was not to be entertained he warned, as she would cost the same to keep as a productive well-bred one. Eventually, I'd spotted Mrs Turner's tiny advert in the local paper, but it wasn't until I was making a joyful post-call-cuppa that I realised that she'd asked most of the questions and I still knew little about what she was selling.

5. First Goats

Mrs Turner was nowhere to be seen when we arrived but there were disturbing stampings, snortings, and some particularly colourful cursing coming from a stable across the yard. It was from whence that Mrs Turner eventually appeared, brushing straw from her tatty jumper. She had the sort of tan that's only achieved by working outdoors all year round and looked like someone confident around horses. Her eyes were shrewd in a face surrounded by dark curls and I squirmed under their assessment, feeling disadvantaged in my denim skirt and sandals and ineffectually wrestling with the buckle that imprisoned Robin in his car seat.

'Sandra Turner', she announced, offering her hand.

'Sorry about that,' she gestured back toward the stables. 'Having a bit of trouble with the stallion. You've come about the goats,' she stated more than asked. 'This way.'

Abby and Tam scrabbled out from the back seat of the Morris and clutched at my skirt. I kept Robin from climbing on the languishing machinery scattered about the yard by carrying him perched on my hip. We picked our way through the nettles and chickens pecking about the yard to a large meadow where an assortment of livestock was enjoying the afternoon sun. I set Robin down and he toddled off to play with his sisters. We had been chatting as we walked. In only a few minutes, Sandra had extracted my life history but all I had discovered, interesting though it was, was that she co-owned a stallion with my uncle, Basil Young. Despite her aptitude at eliciting information from me, I was still none the wiser about the goats I'd come to see.

'I could let you have that one reasonable.' My eyes followed the direction of her finger to a dejected hairy old thing in the far corner of the field, who was trying to find something to munch on to fill out the hollows in her flanks. Her coarse locks hung over her back legs, covering most of what looked like a hand milker's nightmare. It was not the smooth neat udder of Mackenzie's photographs. As we watched, the poor dear made her way over to the hedge, her udder swaying pendulously with each step. Carefully watching my face, Sandra upped her pitch.

'I've not had her here long,' she said. 'She's poor at the moment, 'cos she's milking off her back'. I knew from my college days that meant she was giving more milk than the amount she could eat to sustain the yield, and so was losing weight because of it. Gullible I may be, but I thought that to be a bit far-fetched. The astute Mrs Turner read my thoughts.

'I'm giving her a bit extra maize. That'll soon fatten her up a bit and put a shine to her coat.'
I turned away. I felt sorry for her, but I needed to be sensible. I had waited a long time for this moment, so it had to be right. The skilful dealer was quick to direct my attention to what she had probably intended to sell me all along.

'If you can wait till next year for some milk then I might have a pair of goatlings? I was going to keep them myself but…'
I turned to see two youngsters playing king-of-the-castle on a stack of tyres. One was the colour of a fresh conker, the other, a silvery taupe. Both had the white face and leg markings I knew to be typical of a British Toggenburg. The sun flashed from their coats as they

First Goats

play fought, leapt and twisted, in the sheer joy of just living. They oozed health and vitality. As these were goatlings, I pondered, they were about a year old. If all went according to plan, they would have their kids the following spring. So, no milking until then. That could be a good thing I decided, already smitten.

. Youngsters would give us a chance to get to know each other before I had to have a go at extracting milk from them. I'd hand milked a cow before, but it was a long time ago and a cow was not a goat. It seemed like a good idea and I wanted them desperately. I bent to pick up Robin, an excuse to hide the light shining from my eyes in case it pushed up the price, and jerked my head casually in their direction.

'How much are you looking for then, for the two?' A silence followed, building the tension in the manner of a television talent competition, broken only by her teeth sucking and the tinnitus screaming in my head.

'Well, I didn't really want to part with them, I'd a mind to show them… but, I'd take seventy for the two.'

Something like a bolt of adrenaline went through me. That was the same as she had wanted for just the old dear. Two goats for the price of one! I was ecstatic. Calmly I nodded, agreed I would have them. Mrs Turner seemed pleased too; in the general spirit of goodwill, I found I'd added a couple of lavender Muscovy ducklings, a Welsh Harlequin drake, and a couple of bantams to my shopping trolley.

'I'll deliver on Saturday,' she said spitting on her palm and holding her hand out for me to shake in the way of the old horse traders to seal the deal. This was a landmark day. At last, I was to be a goat keeper. Part of my dream at least!

6. Goats in Lust

The goats soon became part of the family. A shed was made for them in the garden with a yard shared with the ducks and chickens. The yard was to allow them to stretch their legs as my experiment with tethering them on the wasteland next to us that had seemed so ideal, proved to be far from it. The worry that they were tangled, too hot, too cold, had knocked their water over, too windy, had too many flies or were bothered by dogs was just not worth the tiny mouthful of grass they might have eaten before it got soiled from them walking on it. The solution seemed to be to take food to them instead. They played in their yard, and I did all the hard work; cutting branches for them and searching for interesting forage, like pea straw, and hanging it in bundles for them to pick through. This worked for them but was quite labour intensive for me. Thankfully, neighbours came to the rescue, and before long I had the use of a small field down the road and a couple of disused gardens at the back of us. There they had freedom and I could watch them being goats from our windows. I still hung bundles of branches in in their yard for them to pick at on rainy days, just because they liked it so much.

The last weeks of summer passed and the days shortened. It would soon be time to get them in kid if I wanted to milk the following year. I needed to find them a husband. Keeping a male goat for just two ladies was not practical, the practice being to take the goats, at the appropriate time, to visit the male of choice. A

Goats in Lust

perusal of the male goats seeking ladies' section on the inside the back cover of the Devon Goat Society Journal provided a suitable candidate. Here was a stud of the right breed, not too far away, and there was lots of impressive red ink on his pedigree, indicating Champions, which was all I had to go on in those early days before I got to know more about ancestries and good breeding lines. I phoned the owner, Mrs Cross. She was very happy to pimp out her male goat when the time came. Deciding when that was, was another matter so Mrs Cross equipped me with a bit of cloth, stinky from being rubbed over the male goat's head and sealed tightly into a screw topped jar. The idea being, if in doubt, to waft it under the ladies' noses and note their reaction. As it turned out, I didn't need it.

It wasn't long before I was greeted by urgent, lustful calls from the goat shed and an eagerly flicking tail from Lucky, the conker brown one. Both sure signs that today was the day. Goats only come in season for a few days maximum and it only happens every three weeks, mostly over the Autumn months and tailing off after Christmas.

It's best to go as soon as you notice the signs if you want to be sure. A quick phone call to Mrs Cross and we were on our way with Lucky, who jumped eagerly into the back of the Morris Traveller. Before the legislation that followed the foot and mouth outbreak, it was still quite commonplace to travel goats in the back of a car. The elderly Morris with the back seat down was ideal for this purpose. It could be a little messy; even the largest and toughest of tarps failed to catch all the goats 'currants' and the warm smell of wee on straw wasn't to everyone's taste, but the goats seemed to like it, quickly settling down and often resting a head on my shoulder as we motored along. The rhythmical sound of contented cud-chewing right next to my ear and the belching of clouds of fermented grass fumes in my face was all very companionable. We soon arrived, and I wandered off to find Mrs Cross who was waiting in the yard.

Alerted by our voices, an enormous, bearded head reared over the stable door. Cloven hooves scrabbled for toe holds on the wooden cross structure and he snorted his welcome. Alert topaz eyes regarded us with intelligent interest from under an oily mane, while smallish ears flicked back and forth like radars. This was Dougal Humphrey, aka Randy. He was my first sight of a fully-grown male goat and he was magnificent, total raw masculinity and reeking of something like musky aftershave with a generous helping of teenage boys' room. I was impressed.

'Don't touch him!' warned Mrs Cross.
The hand that had been about to scratch the hairy jawbone snapped back to my side.

'Oh, does he bite?' I asked, surprised. Goats, only have front teeth on their bottom jaw that meet with a hard pad on the upper, but they can still do fingers some serious damage as I'd discovered when trying to get worm drench down the throats of my girls. Randy was a twenty stone bundle of raging testosterone. He could easily flatten me, but I'd thought he had a kindly eye and didn't look like the bitey sort.

'Good gracious no! Randy is a sweetie. Not a bad bone in his body. I mean, I wouldn't bend over near him... but he wouldn't hurt you, not on purpose anyway. No, it's just that if you get that stink on you, you'll clear supermarkets for weeks and it doesn't wash off easily... Do you want to go and get your girly, and see what she thinks of him?'

The 'girly' in question evaded my grab for her collar in her haste to leave the back of the Traveller and disappeared around the corner in a cloud of lust. I puffed after the wagging tail, shocked at the change from demure and innocent sweetie to scarlet hussy. Rounding the side of the buildings, I was just in time to see Mrs Cross doing her best to prevent Randy from escaping his loose box. My little harlot was encouraging him, gazing at him adoringly, with her tail flicking like mad.

Mrs Cross saw me and put up one hand in the way of a policeman halting traffic.

'Stay there, I'll let him out!'

I kept a safe distance, watching nervously as the stable door crashed open against the wall and Randy burst forth. He didn't waste time with polite introductions, just got stuck into his idea of foreplay which was to snort, slobber and paw at her flanks, pause for a pee up his front legs and in his beard, then rub his smelly head all over her. Then, with a lightning leap, loins already thrusting, the missile found its target. How my little goat didn't collapse under that lump, I don't know.

After only a few seconds of frantic action, he flung back his head and his back arched. The deed was done and off he slid. I was speechless.

'Shove her in that box next to him and come have a coffee while I write out the certificate. We can treat him to another go before you leave... Oh and you'll need your windows down on the way home.'

Over coffee, I mentioned that I'd read male goats could be temperamental and difficult to look after, like bulls.

Meanderings of a Serial Goat Keeper

'Does he give you any trouble?' I asked; still in awe of what I'd just witnessed.

'If he does try anything,' she laughed, 'I just tip him over and sit on him until he behaves.'

I was unsure what to say to that, so I decided to say nothing. Instead, I sipped my coffee and contemplated this incredible woman opposite me. The protective blue boiler suit she had been wearing was now humming in a heap by the back door. Despite the autumnal chill, its removal revealed faded blue shorts. The look was completed with toeless walking sandals fastened with curling leather straps and hay fragments stuck in the Velcro. The whole look topped with an old body warmer whose pocket was hanging off, but still managing to accommodate a tangle of bailer twine. Her short no-nonsense curls were kept off her face with a girlish hairband, yet she had the sort of build that made me think she wasn't joking about tipping over a male goat and sitting on him. I remembered the posh boys' school where she worked and suddenly found it hard not to splurt my coffee across the table at the image that leapt into my head of how she might deal with pubescent boys.

She was right about needing the windows down on the way home.

The performance was repeated with the other goatling a few days later. Her ardour aroused by the lingering pong of billy goat pervading in the goat shed.

Years later, I took a male goat of mine for a romantic liaison with a friend's goat who lived some distance away. To lessen the travelling, we had chosen the far end of a quiet car park mid-way between us, in

Goats in Lust

Okehampton, to meet and do the deed, something that would not be possible today with our current legislation.

It was nice and quiet when we got there, and we were undisturbed as I lowered the ramp for Ivanhoe to come out and get on with doing what he liked best. In common with most male goats, he didn't mess about, but as I turned to load him back into the trailer, I noticed our audience of a coach load of curious Brownies. I don't think *I* earned any badges with Brown Owl that day, but I'm sure it helped to finish *their* education.

Meanderings of a Serial Goat Keeper

7. Just Kidding

There is nothing more enchanting than a new-born kid. Even a Labrador puppy swathed in loo tissue doesn't come close. Kidding time is the highlight of the goat-keeping year, and for the true enthusiast that hundred and fifty days of waiting from conception to new baby dropping into the straw feels like an eternity.

The months since the visit to Randy dragged by slowly, while I anxiously scoured my goat library on what to expect again and again. As well as my initial David MacKenzie purchase, I now had a few Devon Goat Society quarterly bulletins full of seasonal good advice and two more textbook purchases grabbed hastily from the sales table at the Annual AGM. These were my main source of information in those pre-Google days and could be found dotted about the house, abandoned where they were last consulted, and sprouted improvised page markers; till receipts, business cards, even bits of straw, poked from the pages like unruly carrot tops.

I was proud of my library, especially as both my new purchases had been penned by members of the Devon Goat Society, *The Goat Keeper's Guide* by Jill Salmon and *Goatkeeping for Profit*, by Jenny Neal. I knew of Jill by reputation as being one of the 'old school', typical of the goat-keeping fraternity of that time. Rumour has it that she once frog-marched a group of lads by the scruff of their necks out of a goat tent at a show for causing trouble, her fearsome presence enough to quell their cockiness, despite her advancing years and small stature. However, she was kind to

Just Kidding

newcomers and helpful to anyone genuinely needing advice. Alas, we only met once briefly before she died. Jenny Neal, however, was to become a friend.

I did have one other valuable resource to help me with the goats. I had the benefit of a Jean-down-the-road. Jean was a spinster who looked after her ageing mother and kept an eye on 'Uncle' back on the family farm at Widecombe-in-the-Moor. Jean popped in most days, with an unerring instinct of knowing when my kettle was bubbling for morning coffee. I could almost count the seconds between flicking down the switch and the gravelly 'Heyloo-oo' which would precede the head-scarfed figure as she let herself in the back door.

Her habitual attire was burgundy-coloured crimplene slacks and a tweed riding jacket tied around the waist with baler twine. She was ageless, a hardy farmer's daughter, born and bred on the moor. It was said that if you gave her a fiver, she would find a way to double it. It was also rumoured that she was worth millions but if so, she hid it well. But whatever her financial status, she was kind to me and good company in those lonely days with Mike now away at college until well after dark, which was all that mattered.

Often as she left, she would beckon to me to follow and then fish around in the back of her bright orange van before surfacing again with fruit and veg offerings for the goats, or a few grapes or oranges for the children. I can't imagine she made a lot of profit from her fruit and veg round, probably only enough to keep Rolly, her pony, and the few sheep and calves that she reared in the field next to her house, but they were her life.

They also did well from the veg round, and from stock feed that she could get from Uncle or his neighbours, as did I. She once sent me down to her field to fetch some mangolds to supplement the goats' daily rations. They were under a pile of *'vearns'* she said. I was having trouble finding them, not liking to admit that I had no idea what vearns were, until it clicked that it could be the local name for ferns. Sure enough, there they were in a clamp underneath a pile of green feathery fronds heaped on top to protect them from frost. I cut them in half as instructed, and the goats amused themselves by gnawing out the centres. No easy job, when you only have front teeth on your bottom jaw.

My midwifery experience to date had been limited. As a child, I had guiltily and carefully uncovered nests of squirming baby pet mice, fearful of Mum's warning that the mother mouse would eat them if I interfered, but desperate to see what they looked like. Then later, when I worked at the Vets receiving armfuls of puppies during emergency caesareans, and once out on a farm helping the duty vet with a caesarean on a cow. My own experience of having babies was more of a hindrance, giving rise as it did to empathic anthropomorphism which did nothing to help my stress levels. But Jean said that the goats knew what to do; all I had to do was leave them alone to get on with it.

'Just let 'em bide, don't fuss 'er.' I could understand the logic in this, but it was the goats first time as well as mine. I felt that keeping a weather eye might be prudent. So, an old comfy chair was dragged into the shed with a cosy blanket. 'Just in case there was an emergency', I told Jean, nothing whatsoever to do with my intent to be there come hell or high water.

Just Kidding

It was beginning to feel as though those kids were never going to happen, that I had imagined the whole mating trip. I did my best to keep busy and did have two major distractions, which helped to pass those winter weeks. One was that I had to take Tam back to Birmingham Children's Hospital on the train, for an operation on her kidneys the mal alignment of one of her ureter's being the physical cause of her continuing illnesses. The other was a new part-time, evening job for me.

One of Mike's college friends had put me forward to teach soft toy making to those staying at Her Majesty's pleasure up at the Prison- for which I had to sign the Official Secrets Act. It was an interesting experience just getting to the classroom. Once everyone had gathered in an outside waiting area we were escorted through the series of locked gates and deposited one-by-one in the cells allocated for the evening classes.

My group was of about eight men, apparently all very keen to make fluffy bunnies, and all knew how to sew from mailbag-making duties. To my relief, my job was mostly to help with the cutting out. It was impressed on me that I must keep track of the scissors, counting them out and back in successfully before anyone could leave and just be aware that almost anything could be used for an illicit purpose. The only other restriction was not to use any yellow fabric. The reason being that those allowed certain privileges wore a yellow armband. They didn't want to risk any false ones! So, I had to keep my wits about me.

We had been briefed not to share personal or family details, but I felt goats were a safe topic despite their references to the goat stew they reckoned they would have when on the run. Every so often, one of them would not be seen in my class again. This was usually because they had committed some misdemeanour and had had the privilege of my class taken away. Mostly, I found them to be polite men, who told each other off for bad language in my presence, and who appeared to enjoy my weekly goaty updates.

The most exciting thing that happened during my time there, was one of the dog handlers getting bitten by his own dog one evening, when everything was locked down on rumours of a break-out.

Eventually, my class did complete their fluffy bunnies and kidding day did arrive. My usual morning routine was to get the breakfast on the table and, whilst waiting for the appearance of the children, nip out to stick my head in the goat shed to check all was well. As is always the case, on the day in question it was well after breakfast before I got out there.

It was one of those days. Everyone was grumpy and nothing was going as it should. It was a playgroup day for Robin, and the girls had to be walked along to the school. Mike, as usual, would be off to college. Pandemonium reigned and because of the need to find lost socks and missing books, I couldn't check on the goats as early as usual. I wasn't unduly concerned, as there had been nothing every other day and so why would today be any different? I had so convinced myself that there would be no kids today that somehow even the thread of goo hanging from under Lucky's tail when I did finally get out there failed to instil any sense of urgency. I was so focused on making sure the girls were not late for school that I was in some sort of weird denial and anyway, it could be hours yet. I must not get my hopes up, and besides, I was not supposed to be interfering. They would be fine. Jean said so.

Just Kidding

A restless goat was pacing the straw when I did get back. All was not well. My earlier trance like state immediately left me and the adrenaline kicked in along with my old vet nurse training, as I took a note of the time and tried to assess what was happening.

'Okay'...I reasoned with myself, 'the mum seems to be alright, but there is a kid lying motionless in the straw in a pool of mucus with its head enclosed in the birth membranes Viv. How long has that been there?' Talking aloud to myself to encourage logical thought... and to calm Lucky, I let myself into the pen. As a novice mum, she had no idea what was happening to her, or what this thing was lying at her feet. Although there was no apparent sign of life, the kid was warm as I pulled its head free from the membranes and used my little finger to clear the gunge from its mouth. Muttering 'she *will* be fine,' under my breath, I swung the kid by her back legs to drain the mucus from the airways as I had seen vets do with lambs, then rubbed her vigorously with a handful of straw to massage the heart to get it beating. Nothing. I remembered a trick from a James Herriot book and stuck a bit of straw up her nose to make her sneeze, as sneezing causes a reflex to inhale.

'Come on, breathe!'

It worked. I was in time. She shook her little head, damp ears flapping, and tiny tongue protruding. Lucky swung around, ears pricked, maternal instinct had kicked in and she had decided that she wanted her baby after all. Newly kidded goats make a particular sound, a sort of deep 'uh uh uh,' when talking to their babies. Sometimes, experienced mums will even talk like this to their unborn kids as their time gets close. It is one of my favourite sounds. Lucky was making it now.

Meanderings of a Serial Goat Keeper

Between us, we got the kid up on its feet and little Genesis - Genny as I called her - after a few miss-starts had her first feed of colostrum, the special rich milk packed with antibodies, essential for the kid in those first few hours. You know when they are latched on properly as their little tails wag happily as they suck. It is a sight guaranteed to drive away even the darkest of troubles. I was ecstatic watching them. What a perfect little thing. Thank goodness I got back when I did, a few more seconds would have been too late.

'She'll be fine', my hat!

The colostrum is only present for a day or so. It is a vital power source for new-borns, protecting them until their immune systems are better able to cope. It was my practice to milk a little off freshly kidded goats, cool it in the fridge, then freeze it for any emergencies. I once went to move some on to the freezer that I had put cooling that morning only to find that it had gone. A few enquiries brought forth a horrified teenaged Robin, who had drunk it. Despite my reassurances that he wasn't going to die and that actually he was honoured to have had such a privilege as it is considered a delicacy, known as 'Beestings' in some parts of the country, he has never forgiven me. Nearly forty years later, it is still mentioned with great hilarity by the rest of the family. After that, I never had a problem with getting my children to ask before they took something to eat, especially from the fridge.

Some years later, I was pleased to receive a letter from Jean out of the blue. We both had different lives by then, and contact had dwindled to a Christmas card. She was hoping to return to Devon and spend some time looking up friends and old haunts. She wondered

Just Kidding

if I knew of a local B & B that could put her up. I was delighted to pass on the name of some goat-keeping friends in the next village, who helped fund their smallholding with paying guests. Chuffed to be helping both sets of friends in this way, I was puzzled to hear nothing more from her. I wrote again, thinking my letter may have gone astray. Then phoned, left a message but no returned call.

The years passed. Then one day I bumped into a mutual friend from the 'Princetown years' at the Trago Mills hardware shop near Newton Abbot. Yes, she had seen Jean at a horse fair just a few months before. I can only conclude that my inability to spot a hint for a bed for a few nights caused great offence!

8. Show Ring Debut

During those first early winter months, I would sometimes look at my goats and think about Sandra Turner's remark about showing them. I wanted to believe it was more than just sales talk, as the idea of showing my beautiful animals off to the rest of the world was definitely growing on me.

To my unpractised eye they seemed to have all the bits in the right places, but there my knowledge ended. The textbooks talked about milky necks and silky well-attached udders; what did that mean? I didn't know, and I felt too embarrassed to ask. Neither was I sure that it was etiquette for a newbie to just turn up at a show, and I didn't want to be seen as an upstart. But every time I dismissed the idea, the competitive nature that I didn't know I had, gave me another prod. I wanted to have a go, but how to go about it was another matter.

There were two types of show, as far as I could tell from my reading. There were the casual day-events, often put on by local clubs such as The Devon Goat Society, for members to have a bit of fun. Then there were the more serious three-day affairs, attached to County shows and overseen by the British Goat Society. These serious shows drew goats and keepers from all over the UK chasing the required 'ticket" needed for the awards, which translated into those red marks and squiggles on their pedigrees to let the world know how amazing they are. These marks and squiggles are important for choosing breeding stock and can benefit

Show Ring Debut

the next generation. So, something that was taken *very* seriously, and something I could only dream of aspiring to at that stage. Although I admit I liked the idea of camping for three days with my goats.

With the lure of potential stardom for little Genny dangling like a carrot, I needed to register her. It is something I believe in anyway, and a requirement for British Goat Society classified shows: No goat is allowed on the showground, unless registered as something, even if that's just as a name without a specific breed. Genny had the required parentage to be a proper, Breed Section, British Toggenburg. As such, her new registration number would be preceded by the letters BT. But before I could send off her registration application, she needed a further bit of ID; officialdom, required something a little more than 'the young brown goat, with white splodges that lives with Viv at Princetown' This ID was a unique set of letters and numbers, consisting of seven or eight characters, that would tell anyone who might be interested, which herd she was registered with, her allocated number for that herd, and the year of registration. Once all that was worked out and allocated by the earmarker, it was stamped into the ear using a specialised gadget, like a large pair of pliers, each character consisting of enough tiny sharp needles to give a readable outline, around six to a dozen to each symbol perhaps. That was a lot of needles. This was crunched into the ear like an ear-piercing before coloured tattoo paste was then rubbed into the wounds. In theory, this unique series of letters and numbers left an indelible mark that would forever identify that particular goat, like a vehicle registration plate.

Meanderings of a Serial Goat Keeper

Not that anyone ever physically checked the goat's ear against its number of course; one just kept a list and read them out when required. If you have ever tried to peer into the ear of an objecting goat to try and read distorted faded letters and numbers, obscured by general grubbiness and hair, you would understand why the list method was the generally accepted way.

It was a simple system that worked well, with the added advantage that the ear-marker could tell you in advance what the number was going to be, which made it so much easier to get important registration paperwork sent off in time for the show entries, if the earmarking person was busy... which, they often were at that early time in the year. Obviously, this was not good practice, and it was essential to make sure that the goats were earmarked with the correct number at some stage, and not forgotten about... and I do apologise to the lady in Ashburton, whose kid I never quite got around to.

This laissez-faire approach required a certain amount of honesty on the part of the owner and continued unchallenged until the huge foot and mouth outbreak in 2001, which affected goats as much as it affected cows and sheep. To help keep track of the movement of goats the old system was replaced by the more sophisticated system of ear tag 'earrings' in various colours (which all mean something), that then came into force. These tags are undoubtedly much easier to read, but only when they remain in place. Goats have a habit of sticking their heads deep into hedgerows and other prickly places, which tends to lead to a lot of torn ears and ear tags dangling on branches; but the law is the law. More modern advancements mean there are various electronic methods now too, which are great if

Show Ring Debut

you can afford the reader and happen to have it handy when needed.

Mrs Cross showed me how to hold Genny while she did the evil deed and, as the needles bit into my kid's soft little ears, commented on her good looks and asked if I had thought of showing. While she wiped away the blood and got me to put a generous squeeze of green tattoo paste in the ear and rub it in, I admitted, somewhat awkwardly, that it had crossed my mind.

There was no going back after that. I was on the slippery slope to goat-ruin. There was a new goat section being trialled at Plymouth Horse Show coming up, and they needed entries, I was told. It would be ideal for a beginner such as myself. She would get me a copy of the schedule and leave it at Killworthy Capers, the wholefood shop in Tavistock that sold her goats' milk. I must be sure to enter quickly as the closing date was imminent. Saying no was not an option.

How different my life might have been if that conversation had never taken place.

Out came the books again. The first thing I needed to do, according to Jill Salmon, was to bathe the big goats about a month before the show to help get rid of the old dead hair and encourage new shiny growth. I would need to prepare for this by making them some rugs to put on them afterwards to prevent them from getting chilly and to keep the coat flat and clean. I'd never seen a goat rug before and had to rely on the diagram Jill had thoughtfully provided. It was simple, much like a dog's coat, but still took many trips back and forth to the goat shed with a tape measure before something serviceable was produced.

Meanderings of a Serial Goat Keeper

I had found some soft pale blue brushed denim for the outer side and some of Robin's soft old cot sheets to use as lining. A bespoke seam followed the contour of the goat's spine, and I joined both sides at the chest with a vertical seam, leaving a hole big enough for the goat's head to go through. To hold it in place I sewed tapes following the positioning depicted in the diagram; one on each side about mid-way along the tummy in front of the back legs, and one on each side, mid-way down under the tail. So far so good.

They looked so smart that I embroidered their names in red to match the new collars I had found in Tavistock market. I nearly hadn't bought them because although they were labelled as goat collars, they looked a bit small. I was assured, however, by the man selling them who told me that they would be fine as his sister, who had a small commercial herd near Okehampton, used them for her goats. He was right. They fitted perfectly.

Goat rugs at the ready, I picked a suitable day and armed with a bucket of warm water, some cattle shampoo, and a huge pile of towels and old terry nappies for drying, I set off to catch myself one of the big goats. Lucky was the first victim, placated with a few chopped apples and tied to the fence in the garden. That was when I remembered the foot clippers for her hooves. I needed to do them before the bath.

I got back in time to see her disappearing around the corner of the shed. She had caught hold of the loose end of my safety knot, undone it and was now heading back to freedom. I brought her back and re-tied her, remembering to tuck the loose end through the loop this time to trap it should she try that trick again, and hoicked up a front foot. Her leg was just long enough to tuck it through mine farrier style.

Show Ring Debut

A goat is cloven-footed: two neat little 'toes' coming together to form the hoof, and each soft 'toe' with a hard nail around it. Mountain goats, jumping about on rocks, wear this down naturally, but on boggy old Dartmoor it needs to be trimmed to stop it growing too long and curling over. Not only can this trap dirt which could cause lameness, but it gives a nice level platform on which she can stand to look her best in the show ring. That was the theory anyway.

It is completely painless for them, only hurting if you cut too deeply, a bit like when you cut your own nails. But I've not met a goat yet that enjoys their pedicure. They hop about on the other three legs, jerking their trapped foot to and fro, ensuring that the job takes far longer than it needs to, and causing maximum damage to one's back.

The water was no longer warm by the time all four feet were neat and tidy, so back I went to the kitchen to boil the kettle for a top-up while she kept herself busy flipping my pile of clean terries with her teeth and dropping them onto the floor. I sorted the ones least covered in duck poo and moved them out of reach along with her smart new coat. I couldn't wait to see what she looked like in it all clean. Bathing could now commence.

Bathing a full-grown goat was a whole new experience. I started lathering on one side of the tail end but quickly discovered that to keep her from dancing about, I had to lean against her, pressing her against the fence with my body to keep her still. At this point, it became clear that I had probably used too much shampoo. Also, that I should have worn waterproofs.

Meanderings of a Serial Goat Keeper

We persevered, but with her body and legs soaped and rinsed on both sides... and mine, it was time to tackle the head end. I wrapped my arm around my soggy goat's neck in a sort of headlock and gave the unwilling recipient's face a good scrub with a terry 'flannel'. She was done.
I towelled her dry with the old nappies as best I could then spread the clean dry towel over her back to soak up any further wet and to keep the hair flat under her rug. The rug that I couldn't quite reach. I had to let go. I turned back just in time to see the clean towel slide gracefully off and land in the quagmire at her feet. It settled with a slow-motion flourish; muddy wet stains already seeping across the snowy whiteness.

By the time I had come back from the house with another suitable large towel her hair was already starting to curl, and mud squelched up between her toes. Their final buff up with a drop of Neatsfoot oil would have to wait, but she did look a proper job as I led her back to her pen to rustle about in deep clean straw.

It was a comical sight that met me when I went out later, thinking to remove the damp towel from under the coat to give her a better chance of drying. My rather generous head hole had allowed her to get a front leg through it, making it look as though I had disturbed her in the act of undressing, and the tapes that I had tied under the tail as you might on a horse's rug were wet and urine-stained which puzzled me until I realised, I had misinterpreted how they were supposed to be tied. The towel, I found disdainfully trodden into the straw.

Show Ring Debut

On the day of the show, judging started at eleven. I didn't want to be late, so we got there far too early. My brother Clive had come with me, leaving Mum behind to look after the children, so that I could concentrate fully on my first ever show. I wanted to savour every moment. It was a big day for Plymouth it seemed, as reporters from Westward TV were prowling around looking for newsworthy stories.

From the show program that Clive had bought, I was able to see that the classes for the different breeds of kids were up first. I slipped on the uniform of all goat handlers: a crisp white dairyman's coat, that promoted me instantly in status. It was a shame I had forgotten to iron out the manufacturer's folds which marked it as brand new, but no matter. I was about to go in the ring with my homebred kid at a real show, how cool and professional was I! And then a steward handed me Genny's ring number. Jill's book hadn't warned me about ring numbers, so I was not prepared for that and had no way of attaching it to my coat. The judge waited patiently while someone came to my rescue and we took our place in the ring with the number now secured with a large pink-headed nappy pin.

The Judge was Jenny Neal, author of one of my goat books. Not only was she the goat sections V.I.P, *but she was a writer!* The same crippling shyness that made it impossible to talk to the boy I'd fancied at school also gripped me in the presence of this celebrity; but I need not have worried, she was amazingly patient with my lively, untrained kid, and with a novice like me. She was genuinely helpful. Quietly and unobtrusively, she showed me how to stand my goat correctly and turned several blind eyes to my inability to follow instructions. It was the perfect first show experience, even more so when she awarded us a second prize in the kid class and a third in the milking goats.

After the judging, she came and spoke to me. I was not as anonymous as I had thought. She clearly knew who I was; Mrs Cross had told her to expect me, and it was her brother who had sold me the goat's collars in the market. She was delighted to welcome me as a new member to the showing world, especially as my goats were related to hers. I was hooked.

Getting ready for a show got easier as the summer progressed. A lot of the equipment could be left in the Morris or washed and stowed ready for next time in a handy pile in the goat shed. We did consistently well, yet that coveted red rosette for a first prize always eluded us. Thirds, seconds but never a first. So went that first summer, until there was one more show left.

Totnes show beckoned, and rumour had it that our main opposition wasn't going to be there. Winning that first prize would be an amazing way to end our first year.

It was one of Dartmoor's finest days, as the old Morris carried us over the moors to the show. Mike had decided he might come this time and was driving, so I did my best to keep three exited children from annoying him. The goats were in the trailer, suitably adapted from the same trailer that had moved us from Evesham to Devon. Buckets, hay, and branches for the goats to nibble on were squashed into the back around the children, the dog, and our picnic. It was to be a family day out, a celebration of our first year of showing and life with goats. Pinning that coveted red ribbon above the fireplace when we got home would make it a perfect end to the year.

Show Ring Debut

When we got there, I was surprised to find that no penning was provided. I had got used to shows providing sheep hurdle pens, and there was nothing in the catalogue to say this show would be any different. Many had brought their own, but I was going to have to improvise. It was too hot to keep them in the trailer or van. So, with a bit of ingenuity and the aid of a coil of rope from under the front seat, we tethered them to the bumper of the Morris. They didn't seem to mind being tied and tucked into the hay I had brought for them. The problem overcome, I could go and fetch my numbers from the steward and see about making a drink for us all. This, I thought to myself as I fished the teabags out of the cups, is what life was all about. I sipped my tea and was grateful.

But then a sudden loud bang made me jump, followed by some more that sounded like gunshots. The same bangs made ponies dump their small riders and ran amok with empty stirrups flapping, and cattle and sheep scattered anyway they could. I grabbed the goats nearest me, but Genny was further away. I could only watch helplessly as her flight in wild panic ended with a somersault, as the rope that tied her pulled her up short and sharp. I thought she was okay as she struggled to her feet but then I realised something was horribly wrong. She was dazed, quivering and distressed, and one front leg dangled, useless: urgently, we found the duty vet.

The vet thought that the rope must have been loose and between her legs when she took fright, and it had stopped her with such force that it had broken her shoulder. She was in a lot of pain and because of where the break was, it was impossible to treat. He gave the injection that put her to sleep in my arms then and there. She looked as if she had just closed her eyes for a moment, but it was hard to explain to the children that it was a sleep from which she would never wake.

We didn't want to stay at the show after that and set off home. Mike pulled in for our picnic by a leat on the moor, but no one was really in the mood. I have never tied any animal on a low, long lead since.

They say, 'where there is livestock, there is deadstock'. Death is a sad part of keeping animals, but it is a way of familiarising children with the concept of life's circle. It seems that the cause of the bangs was a ring steward, belting in the posts to make the show ring. It should have been done the day before according to Jill Salmon, who contacted me and asked me to complain to the show committee. It was not the ending to the year I had hoped for, and there have not been goats at Totnes show since.

Although Genny was not forgotten, the care of the animals over the winter months kept grief at bay, and with spring came the next batch of kids and we were able to put that awful day behind us.

9. The New Miss Peckwitt

The reminisce of my early goat years the night before, brought me back to 2004 when I woke, early on my first Hebridean morning. The sunlight streaming through my open curtains, dispelling any creepy corner fears of the night before. So far north, the summer nights are as short as the winter darkness is long, so I suspected it was earlier than my body clock was telling me.

I lay for a while, listening for any sounds that suggested anyone else was up; Miss Peckwitt, of *The Hills is Lonely,* came to my mind. On her first morning on the islands, she woke to the mouth-watering smell of something cooking... which turned out to be the mash scalding for the hens. (Morag, her landlady, had clearly been up a while). Miss Peckwitt, on the other hand, had asked for her breakfast to be served on a tray in her room at precisely 8.30 am. She described her porridge as being made from freshly ground oatmeal and thick rich cream, presumably from the house-cow, to which she heaped spoonsful of sugar, much to her landlady's disapproval. This was followed by bacon and eggs.

My porridge, once I had gingerly reversed down my ladder to find it, was made from the Co-ops best quick-cook porridge oats and goat's milk, which I enjoyed unadulterated by anything sweet. I had schooled myself to enjoy it that way with the flavour enhanced only by a pinch of salt, ever since reading that particular passage of Lillian's all those years ago. Just one small attempt on my part, to be more Hebridean. My porridge was followed by toast, thick, door-steppy chunks of it, and I tried to be polite with the amount of butter I slathered on them. Things have clearly changed in the fifty years or so since Lillian wrote her book.

Once our last crumbs had been swept away, I was detailed to wash up, then water bucket carrying, before coffee making duties, to allow Debbie and Roland to get on with the morning animal chores without their visitor holding things up: we had a busy day planned. I took the mugs of coffee out into the yard when chores were done, to sip whilst we appraised the goats before we headed out for the day.

There were some nice British Toggenburg milkers with a prefix that I recognised and a strong English goat presence. This was largely down to Cad and one or two English 'wives' who had come with him from Janet in Portsmouth. Lineages and family trees were rattled off, but I struggled with information overload and eventually gave up trying to match who was who and just listen, watch, and scratch any curious noses that came within reach.

As well as the main milking herd, and of course Cad, there was also a small group of *Old* English Goats rescued from a cull of the feral goat population at Galloway. Noticeably different from their English sisters, the 'Galloway Gang', as they were warmly referred to, were smaller in stature, with longer coats, and were far less brazen at treat time. I could, it was suggested, pick out a few of the goats as a starter herd… should I come to live up there.

Then, coffee cups rinsed and dogs shut in the kitchen, my head whirling with the shock of all the new life options seemingly now within reach, we set off to see the tweed shop in Harris that was up for sale.

The New Miss Peckwitt

I found in Roland the fatherly advice I was missing from my Dad, and whilst he would not allow any hint of difficulty to get in the way of making my dream come true, Debbie's quiet and sensible suggestions made them a good team. They had lived on the Islands for around fifteen years and so with the zeal of the converted, overcame any of my objections until I believed it really could be a reality. I was smitten and happy to believe it could be so.

The scenery as we drove along through the volcanic moonscape rockiness into Harris was just incredible and my heart was singing. I had arrived on the island with secret hopes that the tweed shop was going to be my answer, but by the time we parked, Roland had convinced me that running a shop would take up too much valuable goat-keeping time. A small bed and breakfast would be a much better idea. I did look around the shop, but my heart was no longer in it. So, we spent a lot of the rest of my stay looking at crofts for sale instead.

I was not surprised to find, as is common with many smaller rural areas, my hosts seemed to know where most suitable places could be found. In between visualising my new herd watching me as my spinning wheel turned in the sunshine, I tried to keep one foot on the ground and consider the sort of thorny questions I knew I would be asked by concerned friends when I got home. Such as health care, schools, and income potential.

Many people I have spoken to imagine the Western Isles to be a dour place, where midges feast on your skin; the idea of living there, something about as pleasurable as stabbing yourself in the eye with a knitting needle. There were uninhabited islands, a sad testament to a changing way of life, new policies, and the convenience of life on the mainland. It can surprise people to learn that the archipelago has a rising population of around twenty thousand, and that there are schools, a hospital, and an excellent bus service. It is no longer quite the remote 'backwater' of Miss Peckwitt's day.

Vets will also come out to you for a lot smaller fee than in the South West and will find ingenious ways to get prescriptions to their clients. Debbie made me laugh with her tale of how some nipple cream for her lactating bitch was delivered: the vet passed the prescription to his brother, who worked at the William Hills betting shop nearby, who passed it on to his bus driver friend, who dropped it off to Debbie as he was passing. By which time the Chinese whispers as to what the nipple cream was for was causing some gossip.

Most days of my stay were warm with a clear, fresh light similar to that so beloved by artists in Cornwall. Perfect for spending time around the goats. I helped trim feet, unblock drains, and once, chased the Galloway gang back home when the call of their old freedom challenged them to escape. Midges didn't seem to be much of a problem either; there was only one day when the wind dropped enough to let the early morning mist hang around a bit longer than I'd become used to, and this was midge weather. Going out to tend to the animals that day required covering as much flesh as possible. Bitey things don't usually like the way I taste, but they were still irritating, with their tickly feet.

And then, of course, there was Cad. The reason I was here in this wild haven of my youthful dreams. He was,

The New Miss Peckwitt

and still is, the best all-round male English goat I have seen.

Even as I write this, he can still pull it out of the bag; winning a photographic competition for Best Historic Goat, run by the English Goat Breeders Association (E.G.B.A.) - even though he has been gone for almost two decades. His good manners and gentle temperament made it obvious why he was such a favourite. He had fathered many kids, not just for Debbie and Roland's goats, but across the island. I was taken to see several of them while we looked for promising crofts.

Recently, the secretary of the English Goat Breeders Association told me that a quick scan of the database showed that there were over two hundred goats where he featured in the pedigree. And that's just the ones registered with the E.G.B.A. There must be many more. I am proud of this. I am confident of his legacy, but it also illustrates why it is so important to keep only the best males for breeding.

Sadly, his age, the effect of the boggy land upon his feet, and his prolific amount of progeny meant he could do no more. That was why he was having one last luxury summer with me, his breeder, - his 'Mum', as his chief guest. What a wonderful life he'd had, and I was so grateful to have that time with him.

After ten amazing days, my time on the Western Isles had to end. My case was packed with a lot less care than on the outward journey, and I didn't want to go home. Nestled among my clothes was a goats' cheese, a present from Debbie, and folded underneath was the shortlist of the crofts that could make my dream a reality. Right on the top, thrown in at the last minute, was my stinky jumper that I had been wearing for most of the visit and hastily swapped for a fresh one out of consideration for my fellow passengers on the plane. Anyone who has been around goats will testify that females have little smell, but the males, as I have previously mentioned, are a different matter altogether, and windows could not be wound down on a plane!

Knowing I would never see Cad again filled me with a deep sadness. I walked away from the goat shed with an ache that I can still feel now, all these years later. He was one very special goat and will not be forgotten.

At Stornoway airport, I waved my friends goodbye with my best attempt at a cheery smile and trooped out of the sunshine into the cool of the terminal. Feeling a little emotional, I hoped for a few moments to collect myself and prepare for the long journey home. However, as I walked towards the waiting area, I was singled out by a stern-faced official. I think we might have got off on the wrong foot, as I didn't realise that he was speaking to me initially and he had to repeat himself. I explained that I was deaf, but he didn't comment, just turned and walked away from me. From his body language, I thought I probably should follow him, although I did hesitate as he opened the door to a side room because I hadn't seen the signage on the door. What if he was off on his break and this was the gent's loo? I peered inside and was relieved to see that there was not a urinal in sight, just a table in the middle of a room lined with chairs. He pointed to the table,

'Put your case there and open it for me.'

Instantly I felt guilty as if I had a couple of kilos of heroin stitched into the lining. *Was taking home cheese illegal? What if he tipped all my dirty clothes out? And my billy goat stinky jumper... please no!* I hadn't felt this anxious since I was requested, over the Gillingham

The New Miss Peckwitt

and Shaftsbury showground loudspeaker system, to come and retrieve Ivanhoe (Cad's sire) who had jumped out of our trailer and was causing havoc in the pygmy goat pet classes... I felt I should say something, warn him.

'Opening my case is not such a good idea...'

'Just open your case, madam.' One hand went to his radio. Fearful that he was about to call for reinforcements and imagining the children's shame if it made the headlines, I thought I'd best just do as he said.

He couldn't say that he'd not been warned. As the head of the zipper slipped around the lid of the case so the room filled with the noxious fumes of billy goat. Oddly, the search didn't take long after that.

I was soon on the plane, seeing the funny side of what had just happened, and daydreaming of goats skipping happily on heather-clad hills. I hoped to be back soon, with as many of the children as could come with me. Sod everyone else, and their practical sensibilities. It was a perfect place for children to breathe and grow.

As I settled into my reluctant journey home, awash with a mixture of emotions, my thoughts turned back to the journey of my life that had led me here.

10. I Had Goats Once

I count the three years at Princetown as some of my happiest. Despite a mostly absent husband, it was a time of exploration and the closest to the Hebridean croft experience I thought I was ever likely to have. There is something very raw about living on the moor with so many charges relying on you, and little money with which to do it.

Being so closely involved with the weather, seasons and nature, is grounding. The reality of hunger and cold, the cycle of life and death, does sort all kinds of priorities. Who cares about the minutiae of celebrities' lives when meals need to be concocted from next to nothing, or keeping up with the latest fashion trends when there were children to watch bottle feeding goat kids and shows to prepare for?

Our basic way of life, and being around the animals, was good for the children as well as me. Always overseen by my old faithful collie Piy, acquired whilst I worked at the Vets, the children learnt about the struggle to enter the world as chicks hatched in the incubator and kids were born in the goat shed. Diversity too, as ducklings peeped out from under the bantam. Her tiny eggs swapped surreptitiously by me for duck eggs as she sat down tight. She didn't mind that her babies were different. She loved and protected them anyway. Abby still remembers being chased by the 'Black 'en' a fearsome adversary who was not amused when Abby tried to pick up one of her chicks. Life lessons learned! We still had our little black Molly-cat,

I Had Goats Once

who had come with us from Evesham, who surprised us with a litter of kittens. She started the birth process in the dog basket under the dining table but after the safe delivery of the first, jumped onto my lap. Two massive back legs were presenting but stuck, and she was looking for help. I earned a scratch for my ministrations, but between us, we delivered a massive tabby tom-kitten, whom I immediately christened Timmy. He grew to be a lovely cat and lived until he was around sixteen.

But perhaps the very best thing about Princetown for me, was that Mum and Dad were able to pop in frequently, having recently retired and moved back 'home' to Devon. My brother too lived close by. I had my family around me again, which helped to fill the lonely gap. Although our landline telephone could only receive calls, (something you could do back then to save money), Mum frequently phoned to check I was coping. When things got too much I would drive over and enjoy an impromptu lunch of Ryvita's and cheese, while Mum offered a sympathetic ear and Dad gave sage advice. She often cooked a roast on Sundays.

'At least then I know those children have all had one decent meal this week...' she would say, as if I had no idea about cooking or nutrition!

I started to make friends too. As well as Jean and some of the mums from the local playgroup, there was Morna; the teenage daughter of another local goat-keeping family. I spotted Morna one sunny afternoon, walking their white goat, Nancy, along the road, and went over to chat. Both of us were a bit shy, but she must have reported back to her family as before long

Meanderings of a Serial Goat Keeper

they invited me to accompany them to a Devon Goat Society event.

Morna soon became my babysitter while I taught at the prison, as Mike was still often out in the evenings. As well as the much-needed supplement to my income it was good to have two evenings a week filled, as they were the loneliest. I would often sit upstairs in the dark with my coat around me and watch the car headlights as they bounced over the cattle grid up on the top road. If more than a few minutes passed from the cattle grid, with no sound of the Morris pulling up outside, then I knew I was going to be alone a while longer yet. It was obviously warmer and more congenial in the Student Union Bar.

Ridiculously, I hadn't thought about what would happen when Mike's course ended. So, it was a shock when it did. Now a qualified teacher, he accepted a job in Bude on the north coast of Cornwall, that necessitated yet another house-move. Whilst I was pleased that he might have a proper job at last, houses were more expensive in Bude and the prospects of finding somewhere suitable, for us and the goats, was grim.

Eventually, we came across a 1940s-built bungalow. It's only redeeming feature was the garden behind it that stretched out towards fields at the back, although I did like the idea that it had a natural water supply. There was room in the garden to build a goat shed, but until then the goats could be squashed into makeshift pens in the garage. It was the best we could do.

It was autumn when we moved in. Not the best time for a seaside town to impress anyone. It was dead and dreary, and I missed the space of the moors around me.

I Had Goats Once

The garden was riddled with rat tunnels and the well in the garden, the only water supply, was dry. We'd been fooled by kitchen taps that gushed an impressive surge of fresh, clear water. What we didn't know was that it came from shop-bought bottled water, concealed in a cupboard, and connected by a tube to the taps. It was, and still is, the most miserable house I have ever lived in.

Mike too was grouchy, missing his student life and hating the responsibility of his job. He mostly yelled at the children and shut himself away listening to Radio 4. What could have been our big chance to start again drove an even bigger wedge between us. Both of us realised that this was our future, and long, long years of this stretched ahead, and it was not an appealing prospect.

I missed everything I had worked for and enjoyed at Princetown, including my new friends, and the closeness of my family. I was lonely again but with no one this time. A lot of things happened then that if I could undo I would, but sadly that magic wand is just never available when you need it.

Flicking through a glossy magazine in a waiting room one afternoon, an article on Woman's Assertiveness leapt out at me: *If you are not happy with your life, then change it!* So, I did as admonished and took control. Which is why we ended up living back in Devon, without Mike, and goat-less.

Some months later, at the hairdressers, I overheard goats mentioned. My eyes flicked up towards the speaker in the mirror, eager for a chance to re-live some of my goaty adventures.

Meanderings of a Serial Goat Keeper

'I had goats once...' I blurted, in one short, but massive understatement. But nobody heard.

11. Wobbly New Beginnings

The weeks ticked on and once the children were settled, I started to look around for some sort of work that I could fit around their school hours. I had picked up some work hand-painting ceramic animal brooches for a local potter, which was good piece work; but I was starting to see trayfuls of ginger tabbies in my sleep, and it was hard to earn enough to make much difference to the weight of my purse. It was time to find something to supplement or replace it. I turned, as everyone did back then, to the local paper and scoured the job advertisements.

I was as skittery as a pen-full of sheep at auction, by the time I pulled up at a farm, just before 9 a.m. one spring morning in 1986. Although there was little to identify where I was, my directions had been given by the owner and I recognised his racy blue and white Ford Escort showily positioned on the pull-in to the fore of the farm buildings. I knew I was in the right place.

The Escort had been parked outside our house a few days previously, to enable its driver to interview me for the position of office assistant for his plant hire business; the slightly unorthodox situation caused because I had no car at that time, and he was not on a bus route. The difficulty of no transport, I had assured him, would be overcome very soon, as my brother had promised me his old mini which he was replacing. I got the job. We had chatted over coffee, and any misgivings I might have had about working at the back of beyond, alone with a strange man, melted away by the discovery that his father had worked with my Uncle Bas. Everyone knew my Uncle Bas, it seemed; a well-respected farrier, and one of my mum's three baby brothers.

Anxious to impress on my first morning, I had dressed carefully and, as I thought, fitting for office work, in a cream roll neck jumper and a pencil skirt. However, the chain on the gate was padlocked which forced me to hitch up my hem line and clamber over in a most un-ladylike, and un-officey manner, hoping very much that my new employer wasn't watching. I needn't have worried. I had to knock on the caravan door several times before a tousle-headed, unshaven, and still fully dressed from the night before Tony opened the door. He was accompanied by fumes of cigarette smoke and last night's take-away, which made me take a step or two backwards. His dark, almost black, hair hung in overgrown layers that touched his shoulders and unusual sapphire eyes regarded me from a tanned face under a heavy fringe. With his swarthy stubble and rasping smokers' vocal cords, the overall effect would have landed him any part requiring a handsome rake or gipsy. I had woken him up from his makeshift bed on one of the van's window seats. He had clearly forgotten I was coming.

A delighted bundle of wriggling Springer Spaniel broke the awkwardness, while Tony put the kettle on and lit a cigarette from the packet he'd sent 'Judy' the Springer to go and find. She had emerged from the depths of his sleeping bag triumphant within seconds: I was impressed. She was a working dog, trained to seek out and pick up for the local shoots, but also made herself useful about the place by keeping track of

Wobbly New Beginnings

Tony's various life accessories, and ensuring that there was never an issue with such things as lost car keys.

I sipped my black coffee, making a mental note to bring milk and tea bags with me next time, and tried to take in the list of tasks, which was mostly sorting out a bulging carrier bag full of receipts to complete the V.A.T. return. Then, I had the guided tour.

Tony was obviously proud of his giant machinery, but I was more interested in the acreage of grass currently just used for parking the various diggers and lorries, and especially interested in the disused calf-rearing shed. After a few moments of trying to make the right noises about JCBs and dumper trucks, an odd comment or two about the lack of a few goats about the place might have escaped my lips.

After my successful completion of the V.A.T. return a week or two later, Tony brought up the subject of goats again. It was coming up to payday. He liked the idea of a few goats about the place, and suggested that, as a top-up to the £1.75 an hour he was intending to pay me, how about rent-free accommodation for a couple of goats

I probably should have thought about it a little longer than the nanosecond it took me to leap at the chance, but I didn't. A week or two later, I was stood in Tony's field watching two young British Alpines checking out their new home. I had wanted British Alpine's ever since standing behind two of them waiting for their class at Okehampton Show, in my early showing days. On one end of the leads were sturdy, four-square, sleek coated, black and white visions of beauty and on the other end, two of the greats in the British Alpine world: Pat Flint and Yvonne McGuiness. They were deep in conversation, oblivious to the love-hearts sparking from my eyes to their rear. As they were called to the ring, I noticed dung and straw stuck to one of the goats' feet. To point it out seemed rude but with a bit of nifty footwork, I was able to trap it with my toe and the goat took her place in the ring unsullied.

That goat was Pinchaford Palm, and I thought she was the most beautiful creature I had ever seen, but goats of such calibre are rarely for sale. My new purchases would not have been worthy to drink from the same bucket as Palm, but a true breeder works upwards from humble beginnings. I was a goat keeper again, which was all that mattered.

For a while, our arrangement worked well, even though I was a rubbish office assistant. I was able to take my dog Piy with me, and Robin too on the days he was not at Playschool. Tony was naturally good with children and animals. He had a gentle, quiet way with him that made them trust him, and he sometimes took Robin out in the lorry when the job was suitable. It was grown-up people he had more trouble with, and behind the somewhat laddish exterior was the soul of a true countryman, sensitive to its creatures, and with a fondness for writing down its lore.

He was also patient with me, and my shortcomings in the office too. Barely batting an eyelid when I ordered 1,000 *gallons* of fuel, rather than 1,000 *litres* which forced him to scrabble around and find containers for the surplus 270 gallons or so that wouldn't fit in the tank, much to the hilarity of the delivery guy… Then there was the time when I left the outside water tap in the *on* position when it was frozen, consequently flooding the area when it thawed.

Wobbly New Beginnings

But what Tony will remember me best for, was the day of the diggers. In all my failings as an employee over the years, this incident even beat forgetting about the *expensive* mare speculums I had put in a pressure cooker to sterilise when I worked at the Vets, or when I took out the small animal operating kit (intended for the delicate skin of cats and dogs) to a vet grappling with a caesarean on a cow one evening because I couldn't find the large animal kit. The resourceful vet had to ask the farmer's wife for a thimble to help wrestle the tiny suture needles through the tough cowhide, while I miserably held the incision together as best I could with my fingers. Embarrassed, I made the whole episode worse by snubbing the vet's offer of a drink on the way back, by way of amends, simply because I was too ashamed of my shortfalls and, if I was honest, a little to in awe of my rather lovely boss to tell him that I hadn't brought shoes to change into and that I didn't fancy following him into the pub wearing wellies that still had half the cow-shed on them.

As far as a self-employed Plant Hire business owner was concerned, the 'day of the diggers' was the ultimate sin. My mistake cost him time, money, and wasted the expensive time of two of his drivers: I sent one driver twenty miles to Plymouth after completing his job in Tavistock, where he waved as he passed his fellow driver returning *from* Plymouth to start his next job... in Tavistock. I admit, the normally patient Tony was a *bit* cross about that one.

'*Dumbfounded that anyone could be so stupid!*' I believe these were his exact words.

In my defence, he wasn't the perfect boss either. I would frequently arrive to find I was locked out, and the keys I needed to get in had gone with him in his pocket, or he had forgotten to take something important with him, and I had to deliver it. Although he had one of the very first mobile phones, it was massive and invariably left in his vehicle as a result; so, although he could phone me, it was hard for me to reach him, and it was often guesswork driving around various countryside locations in an old Mini trying to find him. My wages were not as reliable or regular as I needed either. Sometimes I had to wait until he got paid before I could be, which meant my bills were paid late too. But despite all this, we became good friends and he often popped in to see us - frequently accompanied by chips all round, or a bag of coal or two. To help me out.

I was at the farm five mornings a week, so seeing to the goats first-thing on those days was not a problem. But, having to drive the dozen-mile round trip again in the evening to get them in and settled for the night, and both morning and evening at the weekend, began to take its toll.

The children, tired from school and playgroup, often didn't want to leave the house again in the evening. As the days grew shorter and the winter chills began, I felt more and more guilty at dragging them out, just for them to sit huddled in the back of the freezing Mini in the dark for the ten minutes it took me to sort the goats, before going home again.

Tony was often rained off as the autumn weather set in too, which made working in the intimate confines of the caravan a little awkward.

Crunch time came with the birth of my first kid, the following Spring. A massive moment for me, and I missed the luxury of being able to check on the goats as frequently as I had at Princetown. Tony was supposed to keeping an eye when I wasn't there and

Wobbly New Beginnings

letting me know if *anything* was happening. When I got there one morning to find twin male kids, several hours old, cavorting about in the straw, and Tony nowhere on site... I decided that it was time for a change.

As fate would have it, an opportunity presented itself quite quickly in the shape of a postcard pinned to the noticeboard in a newsagent's window.

> *'Small field available to rent, suit goats or horses. Cheap rate in exchange for help with owner's animals'*

My new goat-landlord had been a merchant seaman and seemed to have done rather well out of it. The house was built of local granite and rambled in all directions, with a gravelled parking area, and a few acres accessed by a short enough walk that carrying buckets of feed from the car was not an ordeal. It was the sort of house that inspired romantic novels, and I was deeply envious. The deal was that I would help the owners to 'get into goats', in exchange for a peppercorn rent.

It was a good arrangement, even if I had to fend off a parade of eligible bachelors organised by my landlord's well-meaning wife. My advice was sought on the best way to convert the existing buildings to make the goats comfortable, and I was able to introduce them to the intricacies of milking and foot trimming, with a nice little starter herd they had found.

Once they were proficient enough to be trusted with my goats too, we settled into a shared routine which made life easier for both of us, as well as fun.

And then they lost interest. We would need to move again.

Meanderings of a Serial Goat Keeper

I had recently grabbed an opportunity to move to a newer, more economical house, nearer the goats, and their rescue came in the shape of my landlord's brother. My new landlord was also a mariner, and this house an investment for him; he had dispatched his brother, Rob, to check all was well. This was probably a courtesy, but it annoyed me. Our privacy and security were important, and it clearly stated in my lease that twenty-four hours' notice had to be given if the landlord, *or his representative,* wished to call.

But I wasn't a rude sort of person. Instead of sending him packing, I felt obliged to invite him in for a look around, to satisfy himself that all was well. Then, to fill that awkward moment when he should have left but wasn't looking as though he was going to, I politely offered him a cup of tea.

A day or two later Rob was at the door again, this time clutching a bottle of red wine. Being the landlord's brother made it difficult to keep him standing on the doorstep, and so again, I invited him in. His visits became more frequent. We even went out a few times on his days off. Mostly just walking around the town but once, a trip to see the carpets at *Trago Mills.* For those who have not had the pleasure, Trago is truly a West Country legend, being an outlet store for everything you didn't know you needed, but never what you did. Despite my first impression, I found Rob wasn't as bad as I had thought. He scored extra points, because he had been born at home on the moor somewhere out the back of Princetown, had gone to Princetown school as my children had… and his parents had a smallholding nearby. Perhaps blindsided, I decided he was of the right stock, even though he had never heard of my Uncle Bas.

Wobbly New Beginnings

Rob lived in an old, terraced Duke of Bedford house to the North of Tavistock, that he was in the process of doing up. What's more, it had a rather large back garden where he kept a few chickens. It also had an open shed used currently as a log store, which, with the addition of a few sheep hurdles could house a few goats. We were saved.

12. Milton Abbot

As the weeks went on, the realisation that we were not ideally matched became more noticeable as we both slotted into our respective roles. I was a few years older than him, both in years and ways of the world. However, we did get on well and I believed that as adults we could talk through any difficulties as long as we were both vaguely on the same page.

The children and I moved in, as being the sensible option for all kinds of reasons. Getting married, he explained when he suggested it a few months later, would continue with the business-like theme, especially as he wanted someone at home during the day so that he could have a dog. It was also the next box to tick on his life plan.

As further proof of his good intentions, he produced some sales particulars for a house in Milton Abbot, a rural village bisected by the B3362 Tavistock to Launceston road. Of architectural note, designed as an experimental village by the rather famous architect Edwin Lutyens, who was also responsible for Castle Drogo, and many other clusters of houses around England. The house and its big garden were very tempting, but I had reservations about getting married again. Mum decided to put in her two pennies worth and resorted to emotional blackmail, her ultimate weapon.

'You're not thinking of those children. You can't move into a country village and not be married...

Milton Abbot

People will talk!' What choice did I have, when it was put like that?

So, married we were. A brief registry office service, followed by tea and cakes at his parents' smallholding around the time of Rob's birthday in April 1987. We moved into the magnificent, Lutyens-designed cottage the next day. It had been built nearly a hundred years previously to house the Duke of Bedford's estate manager. It stood out in low-sweeping-roofed splendour from the parade of similar but terraced cottages that lined the access footpath. Copper rivets held its thick, hand cut Delabole slates in place, a mark of its superior status; as we were informed by old Stan Bray, the village font of all knowledge, who had once lived next door. It well deserved its grade two listing and became ours for £32,000: a snip for something so important to our great English heritage.

As well as being such an interesting house historically, what made it special to me was the garden that hugged around it on three sides. Once terraced and awash with colour, now it was overgrown and neglected. There was also a large shed, and I was able to rent the vacant allotments and old pigsties to be found just beyond the bottom of the garden. Loads of room for goats. It was an amazing place, and we were so lucky to live there.

It was also draughty. The massive old iron key had to be left in the lock to help stop up the keyhole. The key being far too big to go in a pocket anyway, but the wind still blew in through the gap at the bottom of the heavy oak front door, where decades' worth of feet had worn the slate threshold down in the centre. The mischievous breeze then whistled its way through the house, branching off to carry any warmth from the two open fires up the chimney before exiting triumphantly under the back door through an even bigger gap than at the front.

Any draft excluding methods, such as those sawdust-filled long dogs, or heavy curtaining, was great once everyone was inside and the last person in remembered to put it all in place, but during the day with so many dogs and people in and out, it just got easier to put a coat on and light the fires in the evening to make it welcoming for when Rob came in from work.

Some days, when the wind changed to the east, we couldn't light the fire in the front room anyway, because of the choking clouds of black soot that puffed down the chimney and out into the room.

Those same gales also found their way through the airbricks, under the floorboards and up through the gaps between the thick oak planking, making any carpeting not pinned down billow like waves at sea.

As if the drafts weren't enough, the house also leaked. It had been resourcefully built using local Herdwick granite: the very same, I was told, as had been used for London bridge. True, it oozed character... but is also soaked up water like a sponge. No matter what we tried to treat it with, over the thirteen years that we lived there, the side wall that took the brunt of the weather was always running wet or mouldy.

Then there were the ghosts. I would be woken by the sound of light feet padding along the landing. They would stop and hesitate outside my bedroom door. I could sense uncertain breathing and attributed it to one or the other of my children wondering if they should dare to disturb me. I would lay there trying to keep my breathing sounding like I was asleep, in the hope they would go back to bed. I would always give in, of course.

'Come on in then', I would say, opening the door a little wider from where I could reach it from the bed. Silence would follow. Knowing my hearing was not great, I would then have to get out of bed to investigate, but all children would be sleeping sweetly. Who had been there?

Another time, I woke with the feeling that someone was watching me. It was just daybreak. With the hairs on my neck prickling, my heart hammering and trying to keep very still in case I alerted the intruder to the fact that I had sussed him, I cautiously opened my eyes. There was a man, stood watching me, at the end of the bed. He was wearing a khaki work coat, had steel coloured hair, and thick-rimmed glasses. He seemed confused, but at my involuntary gasp, he was gone. *Had I imagined it? Was it the remains of a dream?*

A few weeks later I told Stan of my experience. He looked at me strangely. Apparently, I had just exactly described the last inhabitant. My bedroom was his old hobby room. The little rings of brightly coloured paint on the oak boards of the cupboard floor were from his little tins of modelling paint. No wonder he had looked confused to see me asleep in his bed!

Perhaps, if the man I had seen *was* the last chap who had lived there, then perhaps the 'children's footsteps' belonged to his wife? She was known for wandering around outside in her nighty, pinching milk off doorsteps. Could it have been her wondering if she should disturb her man?

Somehow the ghosts didn't bother me, and no one else seemed aware of any kind of supernatural presence. Although the neglected old walls had a gloomy feel to them when we moved in, the house couldn't stay miserable for long. Any lost or confused souls, stuck between this world and the next, were wasting their time if they thought they stood a chance of being paid any attention over the general mayhem of the children, dogs, cats. They probably packed their bags and went somewhere quieter.

To someone on the outside looking in, we were a crazy happy family. The children of the village would come to play football on the flat bit at the top of our garden when the goats weren't out there. And Robin, especially, would roam the local fields with his mates, coming back muddy, wet, and hungry for his tea. I was never sure how many children I was catering for, but I was glad to stretch what we were having according to the number of mouths.

It was not just children that thrived within the perimeter of that house. The two cats and my old dog were joined by other dogs over the years. One big old mastiff cross from a rescue centre, to fulfil my side of the marriage bargain to Rob, followed by a sheltie cross puppy I had seen advertised on a supermarket noticeboard. In the later years I became the proud owner of the first-ever Kennel Club registered dog I ever had when a chocolate-coloured Standard Poodle came to join the party. My justification in having such a posh dog was that she could be kept beautifully clipped to advertise for my dog grooming business. That she was badly in need of a clip, more than she was model material most of the time, was irrelevant. We loved her silly, scatty ways anyway.

Milton Abbot

The goat numbers ebbed and flowed, depending on the numbers of kids I wanted to keep at the time. On occasions, I boarded friends' goats to enable a much-needed holiday for their owners, or to be on hand for the services of any male goat I might have had at the time.

Keeping everyone company were two donkeys, donated for the children by a friend of my Mum. We had a horse on loan too for a while for Tam, until his penchant for escaping and plonking his big feet over the neighbouring allotments happened once too often, and he had to go back. Sometimes the end shed would house a pig or calf that was being reared on surplus goat's milk. There were always a few chickens and ducks for eggs, and the children had other pets - a budgie, ferrets, rabbits, and guinea pigs lived with us too.

Looking after all my charges, big and small, gave me immense satisfaction. It was everything I could have wished for, and the children grew up with a richness that was nothing to do with monetary wealth. But it was not without its stressful moments, and there were times when 'just me' felt inadequate for the job.

On the day we moved in, the neighbours all found important things to do in their gardens. We nodded to them all in turn as we wheelbarrowed our belongings up the footpath to the front door. The children skipped happily up and down accepting biscuits and sweets and telling them all about our wedding the day before, thus dispelling any attempt at passing ourselves off as a long-established family, as my Mum had hoped. They had been with Mum overnight as she had paid for us to have a night away in Looe for a honeymoon, so they were full of the joys of spring. We were less so.

It had been far from a loving, romantic time. Rob was distant and uncommunicative. He never said what was wrong, but I suspected the reality of what he had just committed to had hit him amidships. After all, as his mother had said to me, taking on an older woman with three children and a menagerie at his young age, when he had prospects, was a daunting thing to do.

Rob's low mood continued for some months, and he threw himself into his job with even more gusto, although he was always conscientious with a strong work ethic. Because of this, he usually came home too late to help with getting the children to bed and would go straight out to walk the dogs. I could see his pain and so tried hard to be the wife I thought he wanted. The result was that neither of us were happy. I was used to talking things through but found communication with him difficult. But somehow, we found a way to muddle through. He was genuine, hard-working, and loved the children. What else really mattered?

Stephen was born a year after we got married, followed by Alan and then Elsie, over the next half a dozen years. I had everything I could want, except time, energy, and companionship. Concerned friends told me I should get the children to help more, but it was quicker to do things myself. Besides, I never got ahead of things enough to make lists and rotas, and anyway, I wasn't that sort of person.

Gradually, as the children got older, they did slot naturally into roles according to their strengths and preferences. Abby, being the eldest, liked to manage.

Milton Abbot

She would look after the smaller ones when pushed, and detail someone to cook tea. Tam was interested in the goats, registering her own prefix and would often help me out with them, and Robin could be relied upon to fetch things from the shop, provided he could buy himself a Snickers bar with the change. He was also great company at evening milking times. He had a tiered range of guinea pig hutches at one end of the goat shed and would chat to them, and me while I milked, as he attended to whatever their needs were that night.

Stephen, Alan and Elsie, the younger three, helped where they could, mostly with the animals. The taller ones could stuff hayracks and they were all capable of bottle-feeding kids or helping to feed round. Whatever any of them might tell you now to the contrary, they loved it at the time! Apart from running wild on the Western Isles, I couldn't have wished better for them. For that, I will always be grateful.

Perhaps it would have helped if we had been able to do more as a family but having so many animals and the twice a day milking routine made that impossible. We tried. His mum had the goats once when Rob booked an out-of-season weekend at Butlins. But most things were shut, and it was the time that Freddie Mercury died, which for some reason, Abby really took to heart.

We tried again, this time camping in Weymouth, but it wasn't a great success either. We had such different ideas of what constituted fun. I was used to overseeing my family and found the demotion to 'Rob's assistant' awkward and unwelcome.

Eventually, Rob would take the children camping for his holiday, and the shows became mine. Getting away from reality for three days with like-minded friends was the best tonic I could have had. Plus, I got to have a whole portion of chips to myself. On the odd occasion that Rob had bought any in the past, I'd had to share mine with Elsie!

13. As Addictions Go, There Is No Better

Goats shows, especially these days with the added biosecurity regulations and form-filling requirements, can be daunting for the uninitiated. I was lucky to have started in the days when it was relatively simple and had such wonderful mentors in Jenny Cross and Jenny Neal. The best advice I could give anyone keen to have a go today would be to join their local goat society and ask for help. There is a lot of miss information on social media, best to ask them that really know! Like any hobby, it can be addictive, but being in the company of like-minded enthusiasts makes you feel part of a big family.

Whatever your addiction, whether it's pigs, sheep, or cockerels, you'll find fellow addicts huddled together around exhibition marquees, fondly referred to by exhibitors as 'tents'. One of the things I love the most about the shows is walking around these tents and seeing the fabulous characters you see there. From the smallest guinea pig to the loftiest of bulls, the people tending them all demonstrate a devotion that is just astounding. They are the salt of the earth. Some are relatively new to the game, while others are carrying on a family tradition, but whatever their experience they all share a passion for what they do. As addictions go, there is no better.

For anyone new to Agriculture Shows and wanting to show their goats, it is important to understand that goats are right down the bottom of the line in importance, in the eyes of the show organising committee. Should an interested visitor to a large agricultural show mislay their site map, for example, it's a safe bet that the goat-tent will be situated in the most far-flung corner of the show; usually tucked out of sight behind the pigs or chickens, and miles from the nearest loos and showers. Alternatively, if a high enough vantage point on the showground can be found, then the goat tent can be identified by the untidy assortment of trailers, vans, campers, and pitched tents; none of which are tolerated in any other part of the showground and which, I suspect, is why we are tucked out of sight.

Goat keepers do their darndest to keep their vehicles on the showground when all other exhibitors are expected to unload their animals and beat a tidy retreat to the proper stock vehicle park, accompanied by colour-coded parking passes that must be displayed in their vehicle windows at all times. But goats, their keepers will insist, require more feed and equipment while they are away from home than other animals. It would be impossible to countenance leaving for a show without armfuls of branches tied to the outside of trailers, an assortment of hayracks, buckets, and bucket rings. It needed to be handy. Far too much stuff to think about carrying to and fro all day. Despite the show usually supplying cut grass for the first day, it is still essential to bring Goathage, haylage, silage, and hay of different qualities, all of which your goat will refuse, despite eating it happily at home. But swapsee's can be arranged with someone else undergoing similar issues, similarly the assortment of concentrate feedstuffs often referred to as 'cake'.

Goats' tummies' taken care of, then there is their physical comfort to think about. Draft excluders that are fastened along the pen fronts at night, show coats, rugs of various types, posh show collars... each goat

As Addictions Go, There is No Better

must have its own milking bucket with appropriate label, and not forgetting the endless assortment of paperwork, both official and unofficial.

At the end of the goat-tent, there will generally be a partitioned off section hidden from public gaze. This essential area is the 'kitchen-end'. Accompanying humans require a camping table, stove, gas bottle and spare, kettle and cooking pans, and enough food for themselves, any visitors who drop in, plus friends and family, for the duration of the show. The kitchen-end is where goat keepers can usually be found during the day, if not in the ring, fussing their goats, or having a kip in their trailers.

By day three of the show, the tidy rows of camping stoves and orderly boxes of supplies have become a haphazard mess of used cutlery, pans, and assorted hecticness, but it's a happy sort of chaos, and in the evenings many a bottle of home-made wine is uncorked, disaster stories shared with laughter, and friendships made for life.

Once camp has been established, and the goats' happy in their pens, drying towels will flutter from car doors following hastily shampooed stable stains and absentmindedly abandoned coffee cups lurk in walkways to trip the unwary. Victims of something more pressing.

Many of the estate cars have makeshift curtains at the windows, as it's quite common for goat owners to snuggle down in them or their vans or trailers at night, but it is also common to stumble over slumbering goat keepers in the kitchen or next to their 'clobber pens' (a spare pen allocated for all such accompanying accoutrements, usually next to each keeper's animals to be handy.)

Robin, as a smallish child, was once so fast asleep in amongst all the clobber for the goats that it seemed a shame to wake him. Early morning udder inspection was long over with all the comings and goings of goats before I had to shift him to get at the goats feed for the milking competition.

It's because of these special needs, or should I say requirements, that goats and their keepers take umbrage at any suggestion of moving their vehicles, and the offending steward who suggested it, must slink away, abashed.

Showing became a way of life for us over the summers, following winters spent preparing for them. The older children all mucked in. The girls organised the kitchen and Robin helped me with the packing. Something I was never very good at, which I'm sure irritated him as he got older.

'Just put everything in piles Mum and I'll do it.' He'd say. He was an expert at wedging things into spaces that hadn't existed until he found them. Perhaps a skill generated by a keen desire to make sure there was no need to have any goats on his lap in the van. As a very little boy, I'd once had to stow the kids in with the children on the back seat. He was not happy with this arrangement.

'Goat's only wee when they're standing up' says I cheerfully, from the safety of the driving seat. Guessing the reason for his consternation. It seems I was wrong, and Robin was mortified at having to wear his sister's pink shorts until his had dried sufficiently to wear after rinsing out.

As Addictions Go, There is No Better

When not grumpy with me for being wee'd upon, the children were useful helpers. They all could grab collars to unload, catch escapees, and were able to help chivvy the goats to where they needed to be. Then, while I got on with pandering to every goaty whim, the children unpacked our belongings in the kitchen and made inroads into the food we'd brought, while doing the most important job of getting the kettle on.

Often the water tap was a distance away from the goat tent, as all exhibitors had to share drinking water from a limited number of sources dotted about the showground. Once, although I had set off with the kettle to find a tap with good intent, I'd got side-tracked talking to another goat keeper. Fed up with waiting, Robin had been sent to find me. Without a word, he took the kettle from my hand and disappeared. He returned a while later, and again without saying a thing, put a mug of tea in the hand where the kettle had been a few minutes before. I had barely broken sentence. There is always so much to catch up with when you haven't seen your friends in a while and a relief to discover that the catastrophes in their goat sheds were even worse than yours had been.

Before the children got wise to it, they would all be pressed into service by other goat keepers as handlers for Best Milker. This is the final class of the adult females, where all goats placed first to forth in previous classes are assembled before the judge for the ultimate rosette and title of Best Milker. Depending on the size and duration of the show, this can involve up to forty goats, sometimes more, with some owners having the dilemma of more than one of their goats having been placed and needing to be in the ring at the same time. The need for extra pairs of hands quickly becomes apparent. Anyone foolish enough to be looking like they have nothing better to do gets handed a goat's number and told to get their white coat on. I was once even spotted when I was an innocent bystander at Okehampton show, having strayed that way as a spectator, and found myself bundled into a white coat and in the ring on the end of a goat lead. It really does get that desperate. So, my children, being relatively plentiful in number, found themselves in demand with varying degrees of enthusiasm for the job.

At the bigger shows, there is a Grand Parade where the top prize-winning examples of all the animals are paraded in the main ring to have their cups awarded, often by royalty, for the entertainment of the public. It's not something goats, or most goat keepers enjoy, and some of the more mature keepers will try to find younger legs to take their place. It can be quite a walk to the main arena, demoted to the furthest regions of the showground as we tend to be. There is a lot of standing around, while the compere gives the audience a rundown on the life history of all the cattle in turn, and how grateful we all are to Lord so-and-so for not only gracing the show with his presence but for winning the biggest cup again, the same cup that was donated to the show by his forefathers many generations ago, and without whom there would be no show today etc. etc.

Having finally finished with the cattle, the voice on the tannoy rattles through the smart rows of sheep, telling us about the different breeds which are often identified by a placard-bearing Brownie-guide anyway.

Then comes the champion pig, who gets to travel up to parade from the comfort of an open-backed truck. Occasionally the tedium is livened up by spotting someone you know in the crowd, or by the odd bull breaking loose and cavorting around the main ring with

As Addictions Go, There is No Better

red-faced handlers desperately trying to catch it, whilst trying to look calm and professional at the same time.

Then we come to the goats, who get a quick mention. By now any of the crowd not asleep will glance across to see that most of the goats are lying down in untidy abandon and their hapless handlers nattering among themselves. The parade is nearly over, all that remains is *The Best Goat in Show* cup to be awarded and we can all file around the ring to the way out and back to the pens.

One year, at the Royal Cornwall Show, Tam was to accept a cup on behalf of one of the more elderly members of the goat fraternity. As Tam very graciously received the cup from the royal hand of HRH Prince Charles for the most prestigious goat at the show that year, some onlookers may have wondered what conversation exchange took place. Tam could only nod in agreement and stifle a smile, as she heard those rounded vowels say:
'I appear to have been given the wrong cup to award. Let's just go with it, shall we...?'
The inscription on the cup read, 'Best Donkey'.
Showmanship is an art. As a novice, I was told that a good judge will spot a decent goat no matter who is holding the other end of the lead. This is an excellent principle and mostly true, but I know from my own experience of judging smaller club shows how difficult it can be to place goats in order of worthiness when they are not presented in the accepted manner. Standing them properly shows their conformation off to the best advantage and gives the judge a level playing field to view them. But there are ways of playing down conformation faults too, and this comes down to the skill of the handler. One of the best things any novice

can do is learn from old hands and see if they can be persuaded to give away any tricks of the trade.

I was lucky enough to be helped in my early years and once, rather embarrassingly, given an impromptu lesson on how to stand my goat correctly, by the judge in my later years. It's surprising how a little squeeze with the fingers here, and a nudge with the toe there, will persuade your potential starlet to shift her feet where you want them. It's also surprising how much easier it is to show a goat from outside the ring than holding the lead right up close and personal, and it's helpful to have an allied hand opposite you outside the ring to give subtle instruction in secret sign language.

From attending shows, you may get to hear an assortment of tips, such as a certain mineral or vegetable that is sworn by for improving the quality or quantity of the milk in that bucket, so important in the milking part of the show grading. Although perhaps check your sources. I once observed one of the stalwarts unloading massive hands of bananas for her goats at a show. Thinking I had discovered the holy grail for the good butterfats that her goats were noted for, I trawled the grocers for years snapping up over-ripe bananas and even buying in dried ones as a last resort. I was the queen of homemade banana cake, and the children got fed up with banana and custard for tea. But the goats enjoyed them, and I gloated to myself at the secret I had discovered. Years later, I confessed to this lady that I had pinched her secret. Once she had stopped laughing, she agreed that the goats did like them, but that she'd had them in such large quantities because her nephew worked at a fruit and veg wholesalers at the time and was able to get his hands on them quite cheaply. She had no idea at all if it had any effect on butterfats.

As Addictions Go, There is No Better

For some, show success depends on a lucky mascot. It could be anything from something always used for the goats, like always using the same type of shampoo or making sure to pack the lucky brush or collar. One man admitted to always having his lucky item, I forget what, in his shoe. A close friend always wore the same blouse. One year, I was tasked with the job of darning the blouse where the fabric had worn through. There wasn't much fabric left to work with, it was so worn out. I was darning darns, but it had to be done. She could not have gone in the ring without it.

My own lucky thing was my white coat. The one bought for that very first show in Plymouth, all those years ago. Gradually, in pace with the years, it became more difficult to fasten across the bust. The alternative was the massive ex-warehouse one I had bought when I was pregnant. I was not keen on wearing that one, and so I struggled for years, wearing less and less underneath it, before having to admit defeat… but I still took it with me to every show I went to. I would have been bereft without its comforting presence in my kit bag.

The showing of any animal is the 'shop window' for the world. It is where the standards are seen and upheld, tips shared, and information gleaned. It is vital to the successful improvement and continuation of any breed, be it a chicken, dog, horse, or even a goat, as well as being a great way to meet people of similar ilk, with similar obsessions.

Showing goats was not just about winning the odd rosette. For me, it also did wonders for my confidence, especially in driving, as I was forced to drive some quite long distances and, in the days before sat navs, not always sure where I was going. I was always relieved to reach our destination and somehow always got there, although sometimes there was an odd incident along the way.

I was once following a lady in a small blue Metro along the winding 'B' road that would get me to the Royal Cornwall Show. She was clearly not familiar with the route and had suddenly slowed a few times as though looking for a turning. I was trying to keep plenty of room between us, despite the tail-back behind us that must have covered a mile or two by the time we reached a nice straight bit. I hoped it might be a chance to overtake; something I'm not usually keen on doing with the goats in the trailer behind me, but she was becoming a hazard and I could feel the impatience of the drivers behind me. But just as I slipped through the gears to get a smooth run-up for it, a yellow BT van came into view on the other side of the road coming toward us. It wasn't a huge surprise that the brake lights of the Metro flashed on as she slowed down, despite there being no need as there was ample room for the van to pass. Accordingly, I had to reduce speed, applying the brakes as gently as I could, mindful of the goats in the trailer behind. What caused the problem, was that the woman in the metro, not happy with needlessly slowing down, actually stopped dead in front of me.

As the BT van sailed past without a care in the world, I gracefully, as if in slow motion, slid into the back of her. Fortunately, I had more or less stopped by the time my radiator grill connected with her bumper, but there was still quite a jolt as we collided.

My first thought was the goats. The heavier ones in the back section of the trailer had cannoned against the plywood inner gate which resulted in the whole lot,

As Addictions Go, There is No Better

gate, goats and all, being flung forward into the small area at the front where the kids were. Thankfully, they all seemed okay. The bumper of the woman's car was okay too, and the only damage was to my radiator grill and a slightly crumpled bonnet. Tam and Abby, who were following in their cars in the queue behind, quickly joined me and placated the poor old lady who was flapping apologies at me, while I tried to check the goats over and fix the inner gate. It appeared that she was well aware of her erratic driving, and this wasn't the first time she'd had to apologise for it.

I know that if you go into the back of someone it is your fault in the eyes of the law, but once we had established that there was no damage to her car or her person, I decided that I would graciously accept her apology and point her in the directions that she was trying to go. As I had thought, she was lost.

I was relieved to have got away with only minor damage to my car and slightly shaken nerves. Never mind fault and insurance claims; she could have killed my goats.

As well as the regular goat clubs and societies, I got myself involved with the Goat Welfare Society, formed by Peggy Garvey. Like many of us, Peggy was appalled at the number of goats that suffered cruelty or neglect, often through ignorance, when bought as pets or 'lawnmowers' by people who had no idea that goats don't do either of those jobs particularly well. The other reason for neglect was goats finding themselves surplus to fashionable requirements, as the self-sufficiency boom declined.

To help raise funds, I designed sweatshirts for the society to sell, and ran a novelty goat show for a couple of years. I wanted to put on something for beginners.

Meanderings of a Serial Goat Keeper

Collacombe Farm Feeds at Lamerton kindly gave us the use of their huge barns, that were empty over the summer and many kind people donated prizes. It was only a one day show with an emphasis on having fun. One year, judged by Gwyn Owen, a past chairman of the Devon Goat Society, my son Stephen won the child handlers class simply for hanging on when someone's energetic young goatling, towed him out of the ring.

Sadly, the increasing need for blood testing and biosecurity meant that the show, like many other smaller shows, could no longer run as 'just for fun' was replaced by stern legislative paperwork.

When I was not organising shows, preparing for shows, or trying to get to them, I was sampling and recording the goats' milk at home, in a recognised scheme that could also win them awards. An added benefit of the scheme was that once every few months I was required to go and 'check weigh' someone else's herd. This was a great excuse to get away and to go and chat about someone else's goats. This offered the same kind of camaraderie as was shared around the camping stoves at the shows in the evenings, where we huddled and chatted with blankets around knees and hot water bottles up jumpers.

It was a world that I loved and felt a part of, and the years at Milton Abbot were the very best of them. Being part of the show fraternity did for me what being a member of a sailing club did for my father. My children have mixed feelings about their upbringing now, as I'd had with the sailing thing, but I would not have missed either experience for the world. I still maintain that we were privileged to have had those unique experiences and memories we now share as a family, both the good and the not so good!

14. British Alpines and English Goats

British Alpines were not even 'a thing' in this country, until the early part of the twentieth century. A rise in interest in keeping goats resulted in the importation of goats to improve our regional hotchpotch of what Holmes Peglar of the British Goat Society referred to as 'Cottagers goats', and others, more rudely, as 'Scrubs'.

Until the importation of the Swiss, Saanens and Toggenburgs, our native goats were bunches of regional 'types' depending largely on whatever Billy happened to be closest. Crossed with our native 'scrub goats' these high yielding imported goats from afar could, after several generations of mating back to pure stock, eventually be registered as pure bred stock with the newly formed British Goat Society as 'British Saanens' or 'British Toggenburgs'. Similar upgrading schemes now exist for other breeds too, such as the Golden Guernsey, and the English goat.

Sometimes, during this breeding up process, and sometimes well after it, goats will cough up an offspring that harps back to their less salubrious beginnings. British Alpines were formed in this way when black goats, with the distinctive white Swiss-type markings, so typical of what we now call a British Alpine, kept popping up from way back in the genetic lineage, to thwart brown goat breeding plans. Genetic traits tend to clump together, and these black goats, were also notable for their size, good butterfats, milking ability... and often horrendous udders!

Meanderings of a Serial Goat Keeper

At some point around 1919, a chance comment by an eminent livestock judge at the time, Mr Woodiwiss, prompted the giving of a name to these striking goats. They reminded him of his old Sedgemere Faith, an 'Alpine' goat he had imported from France. Supported by Mr Holmes Pegler and the British Goat Society, the British Alpine was established as a breed in this country and given their own registration section in the national herd books of the B.G.S.

Why all this is important to our story, is because this happy accident process was reversed in the 1970s, when a small handful of people got together to form the English Goat Breeders Association and re-establish the old cottagers type. Attempts had been made before to 'save' the breed of goat believed to have been most like our old type of indigenous, pre import goats, but it had come to nothing.

But this time they had reckoned without the determination of a fellow British Alpine breeder living in North Devon, who was one of the driving forces behind this new movement; so inspired because one of her male goats kept throwing prettily marked kids with more than a passing resemblance to descriptions of Peglar's 'Cottagers' goats of the early 20th century.

Therefore, we might deduce that the imprint for these prettily marked kids, sporting the distinctive dark eel stripe so characteristic of many ancient breeds, was not so deeply hidden in the British Alpines, a made-up breed in themselves.

A name for the 'new' breed was decided upon, and the English Goat Breeders Association was formed. As I type, the E.G.B.A. is still in existence, although has been struggling, as are many of our goat societies, now that the goat is not so popular as thirty years ago. There

British Alpines and English Goats

are signs that the breed will become more in evidence as its existence has been taken on board by the Rare Breed Survival Trust, resulting in far more attention being applied to the preservation and success of this breed than previously. Interest in using goats to conservation graze some of our sensitive areas could also help to save minority breeds.

The 'English goat' is an improved dairy animal, capable of a decent and sustained yield, not to be confused with the 'Old English' goat which now has its own Breed Society. The Old English goats are more likely to resemble the *Billy Goats Gruff* type of little hairy goat, examples of which can still be found in the feral herds of the United Kingdom and Ireland and some private herds.

Whilst not pretending to fully understand genetics, I had spent so many years trying to, that by the time goat society journal articles started featuring the English goat and their likely origins, they were bound to hook my attention. I knew of Pat Whiteside, a founder member of the EGBA mentioned earlier, through my association with British Alpines, as she was a fellow breeder. English goats sounded like the sort of goat, I noted eagerly, that would be ideal for crofts on remote islands. It was only a matter of time before I got involved, and no wonder that they were the breed of choice for Debbie and Roland.

Whilst my hopes of ever living in my croft on the Islands had all but gone, there was always that tiny glimmer of hope, and I wanted to be prepared for that opportunity, in the extremely unlikely event that it should it ever happen. I still had faith in happy endings.

15. Ippy the English Goat

'Viv... Peter Berger here, we spoke at the show, do you remember?'

The show in question was a new goat section at the Mid Devon Show that year. I had been asked to bring along a couple of goats to support it. The judge was Elsie Morris of the Cornwall Goat Society, to whom I owed a favour.

A year or two before, a surprise party had been planned for her at the Royal Cornwall Show, where she was celebrating a special birthday. Great pains had been taken to ensure that she didn't get wind of the event, and I had made some apple and cinnamon buns as my contribution to the feast.

While I settled the goats, and the girls sorted the kitchen side of things, Robin was despatched with the buns to find someone to give them to and ask when and where we needed to show our faces. Robin, being a good little fellow, had done as he was told and had proffered the cake tin and asked his question of the first friendly face he saw, but his enquiry was met with surprise. The mischievous hand of fate, (or was it those naughty little Cornish piskies?) had contrived for Elsie Morris herself to cross his path.

As you might expect she had no idea what he was talking about but took him by the hand to find a man who did. Consequently, we hid in shame, but she noticed that we were missing and came to find us, insisting that we joined in. I appreciated that. So of course, I was going to support her at this new show.

Ippy the English Goat

It was only a day show, no milking competition, but I decided to go and camp there the night before. It was a longish journey and going up the night before would beat the rush and the queues to get into the showground in the morning. As it was a day show, there was no luxury of a marquee, just sheep-hurdle penning outside. As it was mid-summer, I did not think this was a problem and looked forward to a quiet night camped out under the stars with my goats. And, it wouldn't have been a problem, if it hadn't started raining when we got there.

Help was on hand, in the shape of the show steward who was expecting me, and between us, we rigged up a tarpaulin for the goats to shelter under. I could sleep in my van.

The steward was Peter Berger, herd prefix *Castlebarn*, a man I knew by name and reputation, from his many articles on English goats, but had never met. English goats were a breed I knew little about at that time, but his descriptions of them had piqued my interest. I was pleased to have this opportunity to quiz him about them. During our conversation, I *might* have said that I would like some if he knew of any for sale… How easily these things roll off the tongue!

'Viv, are you still interested in English goats? I'm having to give up… I remembered our conversation and want to give you first refusal…'

And so, on the first of May 1993, heavily pregnant with Elsie, I became the new guardian of Castlebarn Ipomoea (Ippy), the foundation goat of my future English herd and eventual grandmother of Cad.

Meanderings of a Serial Goat Keeper

I often ponder on the hand of fate. If I had not felt obligated to go to that show, I probably wouldn't have bothered, may never have met Peter, nor heard about his English goats, and Cad would not have gone to the Outer Hebrides, let alone me. So, I'm blaming Robin!

Ippy's coat colour was red brown with darker tips to the ends of each hair. The colour pattern is known as agouti; an interesting genetic thing to do with alternating production of melanin and a competing molecule, a-MSH.

She also had the black dorsal stripe and markings required and typical of the English breed and her temperament also conformed to the breed standard. Described as *'capricious naturally'* in the official handbook guidelines.

She quickly took charge in the goat shed, settling any disputes regarding her matriarchal status with a business-like head-butt. If the upstart didn't back off, then a quick nip usually sorted it out.

I got the impression she was used to fighting her corner in a communal living arrangement. Hence her pleasure at having her own pen and colour coded buckets. It offered a similar prestige to those of my children lucky enough to get a bedroom to themselves.

She pulled at Elsie's bubbly curls and often cornered my standard poodle, Milly, pulling out chunks of her brown fluff until I came to the dog's rescue. Dogs were not welcome in her yard. Milly soon learnt to keep a wary eye around goats. It also cured her of a desire to chase sheep.

Ippy tolerated being milked, but like everything, it was on her terms. Most days she would happily stand there just chewing the cud, sweetness itself, not even

Ippy the English Goat

particularly interested in the bucket of food offered as a distraction. But just as I thought I could dispense altogether with the bother of tying her up, her muscles would bunch and she'd be off... with me grabbing the milking bucket before its contents ended up all over me.

I noticed this tendency to 'wean' me, mostly towards the end of the summer when goats in the wild, pregnant with next year's kids, would be naturally weaning this year's batch to have a better chance of surviving the winter. I'm sure she didn't mean to knock me off my little stool in the process or care that there were a few more dents in my stainless-steel bucket.

Ippy had kidded the year she came to me. She was showing no signs of drying up so I didn't mate her again that year, tempting though it was, as I couldn't wait to have some English kids born to the herd.

She milked on through that winter, her yield slowly diminishing as one would expect. It then rose a little in the Spring when the days got longer and fresh grass was once more on the menu, but she wasn't filling the milking bucket to quite the same level as the previous year, again as one would expect... until I was given an English type kid from the people who had taken on my 'ex landlords' herd from Tavistock.

I was delighted to have a kid from the goats I had known back then, especially as I knew the mum to be a prolific milker. Tam called her Morganna, and we plonked her down in the field to see what the other goats thought of her. Ippy took charge. The others were not going to get a look in. Ears right forward, and eyes sparkling with pure love, she approached Morganna with the expression of a mother reunited with a lost child. Morganna forgot she was supposed to be weaned and dived straight for the udder to take comfort in the way of most young things.

Ippy was ecstatic with her new baby. Her yield rocketed over the next few weeks which made not only a happy mum and foster child, but she gained her milk recording qualification (to show that she averaged a gallon and more for that year.) And her Star (*), awarded for quality and quantity at Liskeard show that year. Not bad for a goat in her second summer of lactation. She was a goat unlike any other, bossy, stroppy, and I loved her.

It wasn't long before my English Goat flag-waving attracted the notice of Pat Whiteside. I was taken under her wing and steered towards David Brewer, a livestock judge of note, a long-time friend of Pat, and founder member and senior Inspector for the English Goat Breeders Association.

In those early days of the Association, any goat requiring registration had to pass an inspection by a trained and appointed club inspector. David patiently trailed me around Devon and Cornwall, putting me through the required training over several months, until I too joined the elite few that could inspect other herds. I was in my element. Not only did it give me a valid reason to leave the house, but I also got the chance to be nosy and see other peoples' goats.

16. Robienne Cador

Cad slipped into the world with no fuss or bother shortly before his sister, on the evening of Sunday the 30th ^{of} March 1997. Their births something of a non-event after the theatricals that had been going on for most of the day with Morganna, which had culminated in a visit from the vet.

To be fair, Cad's mum, Melissa, was an old hand having had kids before, whereas this was Morganna's first time, and she was only a little goat to start with.

Morganna had been looking imminent all day. Her sides were flatter than they had been, meaning that the kids were lining up in the birth canal, the ligaments on either side of the pin bones above her tail had relaxed and she was circling in the straw and generally acting like a goat with something on her mind. She had even refused her tea.

It was all going to plan. Yet I felt that something wasn't right and eventually, when my nerves couldn't stand it anymore, had decided to intervene and have a little furtle. By closing my eyes and 'seeing' with my fingertips, I deduced that there was something of a logjam. Instead of two neat little front hooves presenting with a nose resting on them, the first one was trying to come out upside down and back to front, and there were more feet there than should have been. Morganna was distressed by this point. This was not the time for heroics on my part, hence my decision to call the vet.

Meanderings of a Serial Goat Keeper

From the fumes of alcohol, I suspected I might have disturbed the vet's nightcap, and the language, as he grovelled about in the straw fighting to sort out the tangle of kids, was rivalled only by the goat, who wasn't impressed with the evening's goings-on.

This particular vet was not my usual one, although I did know him as he had treated my dogs at the surgery. But he was the owner of the practice and so I was confident that he would know which feet to push back and which to pull on. The theory being that once the first one was out of the way the others would quickly follow. But were we too late?

The danger with a kid coming backwards is that the umbilical cord can be severed too early, with the kid's head still inside the goat, leaving the kid to drown in the birthing fluids.

Trying not to let Morganna sense my anxiety, I chatted to her about this and that until the vet jubilantly announced,

'It's a girl!'

A tense few seconds until we heard that first sneeze and a little cry. I gave her to Morganna, who instinctively made a start on the very important job of cleaning her.

Two more female kids followed, the last one was tiny and had wonky back legs where she had been squashed.

'They'll soon straighten up, said the vet, sitting back on his heels and wiping his forehead with the arm of his coat, mission accomplished.

He looked at me speculatively…

'That makes up for that business with your other goat then?'

I looked at him, not sure how to react to that. Although I was chuffed with these three adorable kids, they didn't come close to making up for the death of Kelpie, my British Alpine Breed Champion,

Robienne Cador

granddaughter of Pinchaford Palm - the very same British Alpine I had coveted at Okehampton show all those years ago, when I'd covertly removed the dung from her foot. Her death was the 'other business' to which he referred.

Kelpie had died a few months earlier, following an incorrect, pregnancy diagnosis by my usual vet. The vet had announced that she was not pregnant. On voicing my doubt as I was sure that she was, he laughed and said that it was Kelpie, she was just fat. The treatment was to give her an injection to bring her into season again so that she could be re mated. Alas the vet was wrong, I should have listened to my instincts. The injection caused her to abort twin foetuses instead, a male and the much longed for female that would have carried with it the hope to continue the unbroken awards in the female line.

There were complications following the aborted births as she never cleansed properly. She never recovered. After too many days of watching her struggle, I had to make the hard decision, and Tom Brewer, the knacker man, was called. His rig could only get so far down our back lane. Trying to persuade a desperately ill goat to walk those fifty yards or so towards his truck made it one of the longest walks ever.

I had learnt never to look into the eyes of a goat as the bolt is fired, but I did with Kelpie to give her my strength for as long as I could. Her expression, that mix of surprise and betrayal, and then her lifeless body being dragged up the lane by the winch on the truck is not something I can ever unsee.

The vet had no idea how special she was, or he wouldn't have made such a tactless remark.

Meanderings of a Serial Goat Keeper

The new triplets were gorgeous enough though. The vet had a point. Little bemused bundles, in shades of fawns and greys and white, with the distinctive black markings, made them so much more interesting than the predictable black and white of the British Alpines that I was more used to. It was a moment to celebrate.

It was while I was off making Morganna a warm honey and oatmeal drink, that Melissa, my other pregnant goat, got quietly on with the job. By the time Morganna's pick-me-up was made and I got back to the shed, there were a pair of twins waiting for me to see. Cador was just about up on his feet and his sister Caelia, obviously very newly born, was being attended to by her mum. Morganna had to share her treat.

Was it perhaps intuition that the English goats were given Celtic names? Caelia went to live in Wales and Cador to the Western Isles. Places which share a similar ancient Celtic language, along with Cornwall and the Bretons in France.

17. Island Envy and Runrig

'Hello Viv, it's Pat. have you got a minute?'

'Yes, what's up? It was Pat Whiteside on the phone, a founder member of the English Goat Breeders Association and an associate during our respective British Alpine days, but now that I had come into the English Goat fold, very much a friend. It was usually me needing the advice, not the other way around. Pat lived in North Devon, but no longer had goats, I'd never liked to ask why. She was still an active member of the EGBA, and at that time, still looked after the registration applications. In that way, she was able to keep an eye on the way the breed was moving forward and who was registering what. She sounded perturbed but excited too. I wasn't expecting her to say what she did.

'I've got the chance to move up to the Orkneys... just wondered, if you were me, what you would do?'

Now, I know the Orkneys are not the Western Isles, but they are still islands up north. I had never mentioned my waning dream to Pat, but I did then. There was no doubt what I would do!

'You think I should then?'

'No question about it. I'm just trying to think of a reason why I might need to come with you!'

I don't think it was *just* my enthusiastic thumbs up that convinced her to go. I think she had more-or-less decided anyway. Once she settled, she found two goats of her own breeding, who were then pass-the-parcelled up the country, courtesy of various friends, until they arrived in Orkney to join Pat. I often wonder if it was the right thing to do. She was not a young woman, and although she remained on the council for the EGBA, she relinquished a lot of her duties and consequently lost touch. The last time I spoke to her, she complained of feeling forgotten about. I didn't ask if she regretted the move, perhaps I didn't want to know.

Pat heading north rekindled my interest in a life on the Islands and it was about that time, again by coincidence, that I discovered Runrig. Not the old grazing rights system on the Islands they are named after, but an electric folky type band, who sang about their island homelands in catchy foot-stomping renditions that would be welcome at any lively Ceilidh, through to atmospheric numbers that provoke tears of emotion. Their songs are mostly composed by band brothers, Rory and Callum MacDonald, often sung in their first language of Gaelic.

I had become aware of them through one of my showing friends, Maggie, who suffered badly with pre-ring nerves. The better she was doing the more she hid in her car and smoked. She didn't eat during these times, and I would make her a sandwich and leave it for her on the off chance she might be tempted.

It was during these forays that I noticed that she listened to some rather good music. It sounded like folk but had the energy of electric guitars and a good set of drums; two sets, as I was to find out some years later when I saw them play live.

I found myself humming snatches of the melodies as I fed round the goats and decided that it might be a 'must have' to add to my meagre selection of CDs. A rare honour, as self-indulgence was not something I did much… unless it was to do with goats of course.

Island Envy and Runrig

    Maggie was a big fan. She was teaching herself Gaelic so that she could follow the lyrics and chat to fellow fans at Runrig concerts in the appropriate language. She had seen them play several times.

    Riffling through the racks of CDs in a music shop in Launceston I pounced on *'Long Distance'* recently released in 1996. Guilt at my rash spending then got the better of me, so I assuaged my conscience by giving it to Robin for his birthday. Fortunately, it was not his thing and so I was able to 'borrow' it back. It was a compilation of some of their earlier tracks. It is still one of my favourites to this day.

    Whilst not able to follow in Maggie's footsteps and see Runrig play at the Hebcelt festival held annually on Lewis, I have been lucky enough to see the band play live twice, once in Plymouth, and more recently on their 2018 farewell tour at the Apollo in London. A huge treat for me. Although I have lost the ability to hear high-frequency sounds, I can still appreciate a good bass rhythm, and as I don't 'have the Gaelic', it doesn't matter that I can't always hear the lyrics. Their music is so powerfully evocative that words are not essential to me, and I can always look them up later if I want to. Hearing loss didn't stop me from having the best night ever at the Apollo.

    Although my Hebridean dream was on the backburner, Runrig's music kept it simmering and I still play their music when the islands seem too far away.

18. All Falls Apart Again

The end of the millennium also saw the end of our time at Milton Abbot. Those last few years as the old century left us also saw the deaths of both Rob's father, who had long suffered from his lungs after a wartime injury, and his younger sister, who was killed in a tragic road accident. He had been so close to both. Helpless, and with no idea how best to comfort him, these tragic events made me realise how little I understood this man who had been hovering on the periphery of my life for the last thirteen years.

My father too was ill, diagnosed with lung cancer, a legacy of his heavy smoking days, despite having given up smoking twenty years before, following his first heart attack. The cruel fingers of cancer tightened their grip rapidly. From confessing he felt a little breathless at his birthday get-together in April, to the terminal diagnosis, took just weeks. I finally managed to get away for long enough to visit him in the hospital, arriving just as he had been given the news that there was no hope. It was the only time I had ever seen him cry, and the first proper hug we'd had since I'd turned from little girl to woman and he didn't know what to do with me. He wanted to come home. I was with him when he died in the early hours of the morning on August 10th, the day before the eclipse, and just twenty-six days before their fifty-second wedding anniversary.

Losing a parent has a way of making you evaluate your life, and that year became a turning point and I

All Falls Apart Again

determined to stop just cruising along and make something of myself. I had previously enrolled on an Access to Higher Education course. I had no idea what I was going to do a university degree in, but this was the first big leap onto that first stepping-stone to better myself and my prospects. While he was still able, Dad had made a little farewell speech to me, saying how proud he was that I was pulling myself up by my bootstraps, so I had revised for my final exams while I kept him company those last weeks, by reading my notes out loud. By, this late stage of his illness, he made little reaction, but I hoped he liked me reading about Elizabeth the First and her henchman Drake. Reading also helped to distract me from the sound of his struggles to breathe. Something that still drives sleep away some nights and should be essential listening for any smoker.

Back home, Rob and I came to a joint understanding. We had grown apart, if indeed we had ever really known each other in the first place. He moved out, and I started the process of preparing to move again. In March 2000, just months after losing Dad, I moved to Bere Alston in Devon; buffeted, flattened, and feeling as worthless as a hayfield after a storm.

The last months had been difficult, trying to support Mum, who had never lived on her own before, as well as recover from the failure of my marriage, and there were the usual difficulties of teenagers who were starting to leave home. The younger three needed my time too, and time was something there never seemed to be enough of.

I handed my dog grooming business over to the girl who had done a government training scheme with me and stayed on as my apprentice, but it was also time to say goodbye to our lovely old Lutyens home. And with our house and home going, so the goats had to go too.

There was no way that, without a full-time job, I could afford to stay on there and support us all. I hand-picked the people I thought would do best by my goats, and those that could not be rehomed were shot by a home slaughter team, who also disposed of the now elderly Timmy, the cat born on my lap at Princetown all those years before. He was already totally deaf and blind and then lost the use of his back legs; it was as if he knew that changes were afoot and had decided that enough was enough.

It was a time of so much loss. Even my old goat trailer, sign-written by Tam and representative of so many shows over the years, had to go. By the time of moving, I was close to breaking point and I vowed no more animals. There were just too many scars on my heart already.

Ten days after moving in, just to add to the surreal feeling that I had landed in some other dimension, I flew to the other side of the world. I had been with Mum when the postie delivered a letter from her brother in Australia, shortly after dad's death. The letter had suggested that my Uncle Geoff would like to give Mum a ticket to come out for a holiday, rather than spend that same money for him to come over for my Dad's funeral. Mum was ecstatic. Her eyes light up for the first time in ages, but then her face fell as she realised it would mean such a long journey on her own. That was easily overcome, I suggested tentatively, and put forward the idea that I could go with her. She leapt at the chance, even though me going too meant that we could only go for three weeks. I had managed to get a

All Falls Apart Again

job, and that was all my annual holiday time that I was permitted.

After years of envying dad's childless sister, my Auntie Joyce, travelling abroad without a care in the world, for Mum this was the trip of a lifetime. A long-harboured dream to go and visit the little brother she had more or less raised because of her mother's ill health, unfulfilled as Dad had never fancied a trip to Australia.

To see her so excited was a treat. After Dad died, she'd had a little spree of buying stuff she liked but never dared, but then had slowly slipped into a moroseness that was hard to breakthrough. This distraction was just what she needed, and she threw herself into sorting our visas and Australian currency with an enthusiasm I had not seen in her for many years. I was just plain old worn out, with everything that had happened, and the house move as the final straw.

The pair of us propped each other up, overseen upon our arrival Down Under by Aunty Christine who was an ex-nurse and of the no-nonsense sort. She 'organised' us. Mum was allowed to stay behind and sketch while I was taken off to aquarobics and for bushwalks, suitably sun-hatted and creamed, because the exercise was good for me and it would cheer me up after my recent experiences. We enjoyed drinks in the garden by the hot tub before the evening meal, entertained by the black and white family of Melodious Shrikes, who also woke us in the mornings with their rich song. It is a sound I will forever associate with that time. It was an amazing experience, to see animals I had not seen before and to meet up with all my Australian family. To have someone else shoulder the responsibility for us both for a while did us so much good but could do nothing for my identity crisis: I was no longer the crazy-goat-woman who lived down the end with all those animals and children. It was going to take a lot more than Aunty Christine and a three-week holiday in the sun to work that one through.

Bere Alston was the best thing to home I could have chosen. It hugged the further-most edge of West Devon, on the banks of the River Tamar. Once an important trading route, that brought lime for the kilns, coal for industry, and human waste to fertilise the fields. Nestled in the valley, the mild climate could produce the earliest daffodils and strawberries, which were loaded on to the train and sent to London. My paternal grandmother had told me stories, remembering when she was a little girl how her mother used to catch the train at Bere Alston Station to go to Plymouth, loaded with eggs and garden produce to sell in the markets. Most of the houses were functional rows of terraces, only one room wide, but which stretched backwards with extra bits tacked on the rear. Built to house the poorly paid tin and copper miners during the mining boom of the mid-nineteenth century, they had long narrow gardens that could be planted to feed the occupants.

My grandmother had grown up in one such house, before moving to Plymouth when she married in 1908. By my reckoning, as my grandchildren now also lived in the village, and if you counted that my father had lived in the next village over, then six generations of my family had walked those same streets. I discovered that I was distantly related to a neighbour, as well as the doctor's wife, and probably many more, as my great grandfather was one of the prolific, local 'Cole' family.

All Falls Apart Again

For me, growing up in Bath, where I had no relatives within easy reach, this gave me a real sense of home, of belonging, of a right to be there. Tavistock, home of the cream tea, was still my nearest town, but on the South-western side rather than the Northwest, as it had been at Milton Abbot. The two villages were loosely connected by the now disused 'Duke's Drive', an old private roadway that had been built to connect the nearby Quay at Morwellham to the Duke of Bedford's occasional Country residence of Endsleigh House, built on the periphery of Milton Abbot.

Queen Victoria herself had made use of the Duke's Drive in 1856 when she was met at the Quay at Morwellham by carriages from the Bedford Hotel and conducted on to Endsleigh House amid great ceremony, with villagers' lining the route and waving grubby kerchiefs. It is said that she expressed an interest in the bonnets of the Bal Maidens; the young girls and women who worked above ground at the mines, sorting the ore from stone. These early PPE were large affairs with a shoulder cape to protect the face and body as much as possible from the flying chips from the stones. I understand that a bonnet was subsequently sent to her. I like to imagine her trying it on!

Slowly, despite my vow, animals crept back into our lives. Mum had started it by presenting Elsie with a hamster. Hamster Mark 1 met its demise from Bessy, our little Sheltie cross ratter. Lesson learned, and Mark 2 was guarded a lot better. Then, came the Guinea pigs. Then the Guinea pigs had babies. I acquired another dog, Flynn, from a friend, despite saying no to it several times.

Meanderings of a Serial Goat Keeper

Gradually I was able to see a goat again without my heart being torn inside out, and I discovered that ex-goat keepers are very welcome at shows. I was able to make myself useful in many ways, from stewarding to handling, or just making tea for people when they were busy. I also did some goat sitting for friends. They could go on holiday and it gave me a needed goat fix, as well as a break from my own four walls. Once I got over my envy, I found I could quite enjoy myself, relishing the old life I'd lived with none of the long-term responsibility, bills or worry.

Looking after goats so set in their owner's ways, when I didn't always know what those were, was not without its challenges, however. The first time I goat sat for some goat-keeping friends in North Cornwall, I quickly learnt that although the owners say, 'fit them in around you, they'll be fine', that it doesn't always work that way. I am a lark, preferring to get the goats milked early in the morning so that they can get out and make the most of the day, but likewise milked and put to bed for tea-time, so that I have the rest of the evening to wind down, and be in bed with a good book by around nine... Ten o'clock is getting late for me. My friends were owls, often not doing the evening milking until midnight. So, when I trotted out on my first day at around six p.m., a list of instructions in one hand and milking bucket in the other, to get them in from their yard for their tea and milking, the goats were not impressed.

As I approached the gate there was a flurry of hooves over concrete in a dash to the far corner of the yard where they stood quivering, bunched together with their eyes bulging and their ears flicking, pushing and shoving each other to get as far away from this scary stranger as possible. All half dozen, apart from one,

All Falls Apart Again

were brown with white markings on the face and legs of the Toggenburg or British Toggenburg breed, but despite their similarity, the matriarch was easy to spot. *Hairy old bag, blue collar,* my instructions warned. Naturally, as boss goat, she was to the fore, and checking me out. Her expression said, *don't know you, don't trust you.* A verdict she conveyed to her pals with a snort and a stamp of the foot. In the wild, the signal to flee. This was not a good sign.

Their yard was central with a day shelter to one side for lounging about, divided by a long hayrack down the middle with a door each side, and to the right of the yard was the door to their night accommodation. Other than few pens on one side used for kidding or ill goats, they were chained in stalls overnight like the old system with cows, so that anything messy drained into a channel that ran the length of the shed. This was to ensure they could lie down on a clean bed. I needed to get them in there, somehow, to feed them their individual rations, and to have them where I could grab them to milk.

I tried edging quietly to my right to open the shed door which was just out of reach. *Blue Collar* held my gaze, the others were still edgy and huddled behind her. As I took my eyes off them to fiddle with the door latch, they took the opportunity to skitter away across the yard and into the covered barn to my left, snorting and sneezing in their terror of me, and all trying to barge through the doorway at once. Having got their night shed door propped open in readiness, I followed them into the barn. Now they shot out from the other door, past the now-open entrance of the night shed. When I came back out, they went back in via the other door... This game of circles could go on all night. They were not going in that milking shed just 'cos I said so', even bribery, rattling their food buckets, didn't work.

Goats are clever buggers, despite behaving to the contrary, and I was just going to have to outwit them.

Pretending not to look at them, I sauntered around the yard, humming quietly to myself, making it look as though I was just going for an evening stroll. But, with cunning manoeuvring on my part, they found themselves near the open shed door. Quickly, I grabbed the yard broom, holding it out sideways as an extension to my arm. With my reach now considerably extended, they decided that the game was up and they may as well give in. I was no fun anymore, and they meekly filed into the shed... as if they'd been doing it all their lives. I closed the door on them in a slick professional manner, just like a shepherd on O*ne Man and His Dog* penning sheep. Grinning, I cautiously peeped in. They were all happily pulling hay from racks, in all the right stalls. Success! Now all I had left to do was milk them.

Milking is very rhythmical, and I often find myself humming or singing along to the swish-swish-swish-swish of the milk jets hitting the bucket sides, with whatever earworm happens to be in my head at the time. This particular evening, having noted that the longer hair over Blue-Collar's rear-end was messier than on the other goats, I revised a much cleaner version of an old College rugby song reserved for away games, picked up by my subconscious and forgotten for many years, that popped into my head:

> *Some brown ones, one white one and one with a bit of shite on,*
> *The hair on the pretty Toggie's comes down to their knees...*

All Falls Apart Again

Apart from my aching fingers, milking passed without any further mishap. All done, and goats made comfortable for the night, with bed-time digestive biscuits dished out as directed, I took a last look at my contented charges. I breathed in the mixed smells of summer hay and old straw that were imprinted in my subconscious, synonymous with happier times. A warm glow of pleasure seeped from my toes to the top of my head. I had missed this so much and I ached for my goats... but this would not do. A mug of hot chocolate was calling, and I needed to get the milk indoors, strain it, and set it cooling. I was thinking about their earlier shenanigans as I flicked off the shed light. *Goats are funny'*, I thought fondly, smiling to myself as stepped out of the door... and promptly tripped over the broom arm extension that was still lying exactly where I had dropped it.

Life went on at Bere Alston. The scattered children migrated back home. Abby, married with two children moved into the village, Tam left her boyfriend and moved into my front room, and Robin abandoned his job in Scotland and made a nest in my garage. The younger children's father, freed from the Milton Abbot mortgage, was able to buy a house in the village equidistant between his children and me, and his mother. And so it was; a time to mend and re-group.

The greys of my existence slowly regained their colour. I was getting back on my feet. A friend had bullied me into going with her to a dance to celebrate the summer solstice of 2000, where I met a new man. The timing seemed significant, meant to be even, and over the next four years that Paul and I saw each other, I had the sort of fun I'd missed out on as a teenager. We renovated

Mum and Dad's old boat that was rotting in the hedge and took it with us on camping trips with the younger children. We went surfing, and I even went out in the evening sometimes. He rebuilt my confidence, and with that came hope. Going full circle, I started an Honours degree at the College of St Mark and St John, where Mike had done his degree all those years before. I was determined to be qualified and get a decently paid job so that I could support my children. I wanted to be able to give them the things their father did, more than that, I wanted them to be proud of me.

And then Mum became ill.

She had fallen in Melbourne. She said she had tripped, but on reflection, I think it may have been the first of many mini strokes that she was to have over the following months. She was then diagnosed with cancer, and then a brain tumour... Then came the phone call for me to go with her in the ambulance to Derriford hospital, where I sat with her, holding her hand until she quietly closed her eyes for good.

Numb once more, my relationship with Paul floundered. He will always be one of the great loves of my life, but I was emotionally exhausted, and I could no longer be his 'Mum' too; a role I felt I had increasingly slipped into. I needed someone to support me now, and that was something, with the extent of his own issues, that he was not able to do.

Once again, it was just me and the kids. I did not even have the motivation to go back and finish the last two semesters of the degree that I had interrupted to look after Mum. I mourned for everything I had lost,

All Falls Apart Again

especially Mum. It felt as though things could not get much worse.

Which is where I was at when Roland rang with his invitation to come to the Hebrides and see Cad for his last luxury summer. It was such an unlikely thing to happen. How often does anyone have a stranger ring them up, to invite them to the very place they have had a long-term unrequited love affair with? Such an opportunity at that time felt like fate to me.

19. Heading North

I was thankful that there had been no repercussions from the bag search at Stornoway Airport on my way home from Debbie and Roland's and I was wildly excited at the prospect of moving up there with my children. As I settled myself on the plane travelling back south, I knew the next logical step was to take them to the Hebrides for a visit as soon as I could arrange it. I wanted them to see it for themselves, convinced they would fall in love with it as deeply as I had. I was blind to any potential problems; carried along on a tide of euphoric enthusiasm for the future. I had swung from the deeply depressed pre-Hebrides me, to a new wildly happy version of me that I hardly recognised. I hadn't felt this level of pure joy for many years. The Hebrides would be my respite cure just as sure as they had been for Miss Peckwitt. Those Western Isles were going to save me.

Back home, some of my friends voiced their doubts; but I was determined, it was my destiny, I was sure. I re-read my Lillian Beckwith books, feeling a fond empathy with the way the islanders teased the long-suffering English Miss Peckwitt and her attempts to adapt to crofting life, imagining myself as her.

My waking hours were now spent daydreaming about the goats I had picked out from Debbie and Roland's herd, consumed with thinking about which male I would use to build my future gene-line and wishing I had taken more photographs of them to refer to. And, as the Sandman caressed my eyes each night, I smiled

Heading North

at the perfect show-stopping kids I would have... Ignoring the fact that there were no specialist goat shows on any of the Islands at which to show them.

Only three of my six children could make the trip at such short notice, which was still too many of us to land upon the good nature of my friends and their small croft. Undeterred, I booked accommodation near the airport and hired us car. With the cost of the airfare for the four of us now rivalling the price I'd paid to go to Australia, plus the accommodation, the hire car, and money set aside for food, the costs were ridiculous for only a weekend away; but, I argued, it had to be done. It was important for the children to see their new home and to understand why I was so smitten. I was off my head with excitement, and already planning a future trip with the next consignment of children when we had more time to plan.

We were all jaded by the time we landed at Stornoway airport that evening and looking forward to finding our accommodation and getting the kettle on for a proper cup of tea to revive our flagging spirits. Six o'clock that same morning seemed like a long time ago, and I was struggling with the effort of shepherding my little flock.

The car hire company was happily located at the airport, and it didn't take long to take possession of the little lime green car... which immediately identified us as tourists. Tam argued that she should be the designated driver.

'Mum, just because there is only one road, doesn't mean you won't get us lost... we all just want to get there, don't we?' Nods of agreement came from the younger two, as Tam climbed into the driving seat, and

Alan took charge of navigation. Their lack of faith stemming from their experiences of accompanying me over too many years while trying to find far-flung goat-places, mostly found at the end of un-marked grass-centred tracks. We did a quick trolly dash around the Co-op before we left Stornoway, then set off to our temporary home as the sun began to set.

Our accommodation, we were told in the instructions I'd been given, was a single-storey house, about half a mile from the airport, going by name of *The Plough*. It shouldn't be too difficult to find. After all it was not as if we were trying to find somewhere in a place as hectic as the middle of London, for example.

'Look for a "wee plough in the hedge"', I instructed helpfully from the passenger seat, reading from the letter I clutched from our accommodation provider. But, despite driving up and down the *only* road several times, there were no ploughs to be seen, wee or otherwise. As the light was fading, tempers began to get short. This was not the plan. I wanted every moment to be remembered as blissfully happy. I was getting desperate: *it had to be here somewhere!*

'Ask that man, Mum.' Alan suggested, on our third sweep.

'Okay', I replied, fumbling with my seatbelt. Before I was unbuckled, Tam had pulled over, leapt out, and was already assailing the man herself. They were too far away to hear what was being said, but he looked puzzled, and there was a lot of arm-waving. Eventually, he turned and walked into his house... with my daughter following.

After several minutes I thought that I should probably go and see what had happened to my second eldest. She had been gone quite a long time: what if he was chopping her into little pieces, while we were sat in the

Heading North

car playing eye-spy? Leaving Elsie and Alan in the car, I hurried along the path and knocked politely on the open door. I was relieved that, instead of a crazed Hebridean clutching a bloodied axe, a tiny, aproned figure appeared in the door frame, wisps of silver streaking her face as the easterly wind made its presence felt. I explained that I was looking for my daughter, last seen entering this very house. Concerned that I might offend, I tried not to make it sound like an accusation.

'Aye, come away in dear… Would you like a wee cup of tea? Some cake? My husband is just finding the map.'… was that a euphemism for murder weapon I wondered?

Alan had joined us by this time, ever helpful, bringing with him our written instructions that I had left in the car. As soon as they saw the name of the owner they knew exactly where it was. They hadn't recognised it by its fancy English name of *'The Plough'*. Crofting communities were small. The owner's name was enough. Complex addresses were not required.

Managing to stop the kind-hearted lady before she sat us all down for tea and cake, we thanked them, and made our way back to a wide-eyed Elsie, who seeing us all disappearing one at a time into a stranger's house like something from a Brian Rix farce, had been concerned that she might be the next victim. Having reassured her that we were all fine, we pottered on down the road… and there it was.

Peeping out from deep within a tangle of stone, ivy, and other hedgerow plants, was a single plough tine - which offered just enough of a flat surface to have the inscription *'The Plough'* hand-painted in dirtied wobbly-white letters. This was nothing like the old hand-ploughs of the West County pub-garden variety that we had mistakenly been looking for. Thankfully, the key was under the doormat as per our instructions, so while the children decided on their bedrooms, I got the kettle boiling. I needed that cup of tea. Indeed, if I was a drinker, a wee dram of the hard stuff would not have gone amiss.

We arrived late on Saturday and had two whole days of Hebridean bliss to enjoy. Monday, we agreed, we would be tourists and find the Neolithic standing stones at Callanish, believed to predate Stonehenge, which had always held me spellbound. I was keen to see them too, as they were supposed to have a connection with standing stones the younger two children and I had recently seen in Brittany. Our sightseeing day could also incorporate the Arnol Blackhouses and Museum which were on that side of the island, and I hoped we would have time to visit the interesting beehive-shaped structure known as a *Broch* while we were over there. But tomorrow was Sunday. A day still respected on the islands as a religious day. A traditional day of rest and a time for reflection, and therefore, the best day to slip out and go and see the croft-land that I had singled out as our potential new home.

As it was a Sunday, all facilities and shops would be shut, so it was essential to take anything we might need with us. I wanted the day to be perfect and took great pains with the picnic to include everyone's favourites. Tam buttered bread rolls, keeping some plain to add cheese and onion crisps to (which was her penchant), filling the others with cheese or tuna satisfying the rest of us. We had bought a giant selection-bag of crisps, but with the cheese and onion gone for Tam's rolls, and

Heading North

the 'pink' ones allocated to Elsie (the only ones she would eat), Alan and I would have to fight it out over the salt and vinegar or be stuck with the plain. There was also a packet of wafer-thin ham, again with Elsie in mind, bananas and apples for the token healthy option, and lastly, as a special treat and one usually reserved for birthdays, Cadbury's chocolate fingers. I really wanted the day to be memorable.

As sporty-Alan filled his water bottle, I made some tea to fill the large flask we had found in a cupboard. We were now nearly ready to go, all that remained to do was to call Elsie in from playing outside.

'Right, come on then. Let's get this show on the road! Elsie, get your trainers on.'

'I can't. They're wet... The grass was wet.' She explained in response to my arched eyebrows.

'Have you got anything else you could wear?'

'No.' Her lower lip began to pout, and I knew better than to argue: Nothing was going to induce Elsie to put wet trainers on. I was stood looking at her in despair, wondering how to get over this one, when Alan appeared waving a pair of wellies, approximately Elsie's size.

'I found these in the cupboard...' He offered them towards Elsie. Her nose wrinkled.

'I'm not wearing *those*.'

My youngest daughter can be stubborn. I've no idea who she gets it from.

'What's wrong with them?' I asked, although I already knew the answer. They had had someone else's feet in them and had clearly been in the cupboard a while. Her face was contorted with conflicting emotions.

'They've got spiders in them.'

I knew that no amount of shaking them was going to convince her otherwise. She had made up her mind.

There was a pause while this half of the stalemate considered the options. One thing having several children does, is to teach you to pick your battles; I recognised this was one that I had no chance of winning. I backed down.

'Okay… just make sure you have a change of socks. I'll carry you to the car and we can put your trainers in the sun on the back window. They'll be dry by the time we get there. Right,' I chivvied and tried again, 'let's go!'

I piggy-backed Elsie to the car and dumped her in the back. Tam had the engine running, I jumped in... finally, we were off on our adventure.

Yesterday's clouds had trundled off to reveal the sun that had been waiting for its opportunity to give us the best day ever. Elsie's trainers steamed as Tam drove, and ever-capable Alan, captain of the Tavistock junior football team and leader of Dartmoor Ten Tors Challenge groups, again, slotted naturally into his role as map-reader.

I relaxed my shoulders and sat back to enjoy a day out on the brink of our new lives. Elsie seemed cautiously impressed with the village school she would be attending as we drove by, and I casually talked with Alan about his options at the Nicholson Institute in Stornoway. Tam had already been assigned as 'management' of the B&B we were going to have built... which meant I could play with my goats and potter. Perfect. The land I had my eye on, and my grandiose ambition, had room enough for everyone, including those left behind this time.

Heading North

We joined the single-lane road that trundled down through the nearby village, took a right turn, and followed the loch alongside a salmon farm. The road continued, climbed steadily past a petering of houses, before what little civilisation there was, left us on our own with just the moorland, sky, and the dark-peaty waters of the loch below us for company.

What seemed like ages after leaving *'The Plough'* we arrived at a parcel of bare-land croft, on a far headland to the right of Loch Grimshader, or Loch Griomsiadair if you 'have the Gaelic'. There was no actual inhabitable dwelling on the land, just the ruins of an old blackhouse.

The road bisected the land I wanted, with the bulk of the grazing land to the left that sloped gently down to the water's edge. The land to the right, was where the tumbled ruins of the old blackhouse and byre were, surrounded by enough space for us to have a comfortable place to live.

It was so empty and spacious that it was difficult to imagine the landscape as looking any different; there was so much wild beauty around, that the idea of a brand-new house and so much new activity seemed almost disrespectful, somehow. I wanted to tell the ghosts of the blackhouse-past that I meant well, and despite my Englishness, I would value what they had no doubt been forced to leave. I wanted to reassure them I was worthy.

We decided to explore, and instinctively we all headed towards water. Elsie's wet feet no longer mattered; we soon all had soggy feet as we hopped from one tuffet of reeds to another and made our way to the edge of the sea-loch. We sat for a long time, sharing the water from Alan's bottle, and exclaiming about how stunning the scenery was. When we ran out of adjectives, we made our way back to the car. It was time to find somewhere for our picnic.

Happy, but hungry, we drove on. Spoilt with so many beautiful views, it was hard to select the exact spot to stop. Eventually, we decided upon a gravelled pull in that was clearly intended for such a purpose, and it offered us the perfect backdrop for munching our goodies. I had built up the anticipation of our meal by mentioning the favourite foods, saving the chocolate fingers as a sort of drum roll as we pulled in. Eagerly, I leapt out to get the food and drink from the boot... only, it wasn't there. I stared at the empty space for a moment or two, willing the food to appear, but it didn't: I had forgotten the picnic.

There was no coming back from that one. Miles from 'home' and nowhere open because it was Sunday, we had no option but to head back. Everyone was very quiet, apart from the occasional grumble of both tummies and vocal cords. This was not the perfect day I had planned.

Too soon it was time to pack our things and head back to the airport. We gave back the keys of the little green car and took our seats while we waited to be called for boarding. It was then I discovered I had forgotten my favourite hat, and I was loath to leave it behind. Alan, being the athletic one, volunteered to sprint back to our accommodation and retrieve it; the key having been put back under the mat as we had been instructed. He only just made it back in time to board. I'm not quite sure what I would have done if he hadn't.

We were all tired as we took our seats on the plane and made our way back home. I could tell that despite

Heading North

saving the day, Alan was experiencing massive inner turmoil about the decision he was being asked to make, the life that I was asking him to give up. The long journey gave me plenty of time for reflection too, his anguish making me face the 'what if's' that I had not allowed myself to acknowledge before. Most importantly, *what if* Abby's husband said no? *What if* some came, and some didn't. What about their Dads? How would I feel about splitting the family?

'You will come home Mum, won't you?'

Abby's heartfelt plea still haunted me. *What was I thinking of?* I was not free to up-sticks and go. I tried to bury my silent heartbreak as reality confronted me and I realised that this Hebridean dream of mine was not meant to be... As before when things got tough, I must pick myself up, square my shoulders, and come up with an alternative plan. I still clung to the hope that one day I would call the Islands 'home' but had to accept that now was not the time.

20. The Alternative Plan

As Fate would have it, it didn't take me long to come up with a 'Plan B', courtesy of Mum's estate. Although my much healthier bank balance could have just about stretched to a modest little croft on the Hebrides, it was nothing like enough for a smallholding in the Southwest. But..., as the local estate agent suggested, it might buy me a small piece of land. I started looking, but without much luck and then one day...

'Do goats eat trees?' Martin, the estate agent asked.

'Yes,' I said. 'They demolish them with relish... Why?'

'A small bit of land has come up for sale close by... you could even walk to it from where you are. It's not had anything done to it for years and the trees have self-seeded. It's such a jungle that I can't even get in there to verify the measurements, but working off the map, it's about three-quarters of an acre... would that do?'

'When can I see it!'

'Any time you like... Out of your road, straight across at the crossroads, and down the hill. It's the broken gate buried in the hedge on the left.... I'll email the details across now.'

Excited, I called Abby to ask if she wanted to come with me. I didn't need to ask twice. She found me already outside, notebook in hand, impatiently hopping about outside my front door.

We found the gate Martin had broken, forcing it open to get in, and immediately discovered that he was right about the impenetrable jungle of brambles and young trees too. That didn't stop my excited squawks though,

The Alternative Plan

as I pushed my way in, and discovered a ramshackle tin shed that would be big enough for a couple of goats, until something more permanent could be arranged.

Three-quarters of an acre was smaller than ideal, but as I had given up hope of finding anywhere, and this was so close to the house, there was no doubt in my mind about wanting it. I had kept goats on a lot less. And, it had trees. I was overjoyed at the thought of owning trees.

I stood for a moment, allowing the sense of the place to sink in. Obscured by oak, hazel, ash, alder and even a holm oak, the land gently sloped south towards where I knew the River Tamar meandered lazily, marking the boundary between Devon and Cornwall. I knew too that nearby were the remains of engine houses and the towering stacks of the valley's mining heritage, and that Morwellham Quay, Cotehele, and Calstock, were all down along the river below me somewhere. Everything that made it home for me. I absolutely loved it.

'The goats can clear the tangle,' I remarked, thinking out loud.

'Tanglewood' quipped Abby, by way of reply, and it was known as Tanglewood ever after.

The only drawback was, that it wasn't mine yet. It was being sold by informal tender, the cruellest of all ways to purchase anything. A secret ballot, where each sealed bid would be handed over to the Estate Agents to be opened at the appointed date and time by the Vendor, was going to determine my destiny. It was not necessarily the highest bid that would secure it either; Martin explained, rather unhelpfully. Because the vendor lived locally, he wanted his land to go to the 'right' person. So, as the closing date was 17th September at noon, I had a month to come up with a paragraph or two on why I wanted the land, and what I would use it for as well as agonise over how much to offer as my bid.

Martin's' advice was not much help. 'Just ask yourself, how much would it be worth to you, and can you afford that? Make it an odd amount, it can make all the difference if there are a lot of bids around the same amount.'

This was so hard to do and writing those few paragraphs, that were so important, was worse than any personal statement on any job application I had ever done. After many false starts I decided that a formal approach was just not working. I started again, this time just letting the words flow from my soul and hoping that my honesty would win the vendor's heart. I gave my sealed envelope a kiss and wished it luck as I popped it though Mansbridge Balment's letter box to take its chance. I could do no more but wait.

I'd had to give up my degree to look after Mum towards the end of her life, on her doctor's orders, but I had kept a part time job at the nearby living history museum of Morwellham Quay, taking the place of Tam, who was leaving. I had started in Tam's old role as a costumed interpreter, giving talks about the place to both visiting parties of schoolchildren and members of the public. By the time the field had come up for sale, I was part of the management team and a buyer for the Victorian-themed shop that I now ran. My uniform was a Victorian outfit with a crinoline, that unhelpfully swept things off shelves as I walked past, especially made for me by the museum's seamstress.

The Alternative Plan

I was very proud of my shop. From behind my counter, I could gaze with pleasure at shelves neatly stocked with beautiful things that I had selected and ordered. The top shelves held museum artefacts, rows of copper kettles and pans, coils of sisal rope made at Morwellham on the rope walk, along with bottles and jars and old-ship's lights. Behind me, in rows of traditional glass jars, were sweets that evoked exclamations of delight and many childhood tales from visitors as I measured out sherbet lemons and aniseed balls onto the balance scales before deftly twisting closed the paper bags. Bags that I had sourced and had printed with an old Morwellham logo. From where I stood, I could look out and see the Tamar River flowing toward Gunnislake and on to Plymouth. Right in the middle of the shop, gracing the polished oak floorboards with his beauty was Rocky Rocking Horse. An ethereal, dappled, bespoke creature with flowing mane and tail that little girls loved to brush with his personal grooming kit. At over a thousand pounds it would have taken one very special customer to buy him, which was highly unlikely, but I lived in hope, and as he had come to live with us on sale or return terms, it didn't really matter. He looked good and captured the essence of Victorian childhoods.

But times were not good for Morwellham. It was a charity, and no longer attracting the visitor numbers that it had enjoyed when it first opened in the 1970s. So, it wasn't well paid, but it was just about enough and the financial shortcomings were offset by it being a unique place to work, with the bonus of having immensely beautiful and historic surroundings. For the first time in a long while, I felt like I was managing. I had an income, a house, and if the fates were kind to me on the 17th of September, the disappointment of my crushed dream might be assuaged, and I could have goats again.

When the 17th finally arrived, I was more of a jittering wreck than my first day at my new job with the Plant Hire firm. All my hopes rested on this.

Abby sat with me as the hands on my Ikea kitchen clock, ticked their way towards midday… and went past. Normally stoic about whatever was being decided for me by the powers' unseen, I wasn't this time. I wasn't sure I could cope with the disappointment if my bid wasn't good enough, especially after a month of confidently affirming to myself that it was going to be mine. As the seconds past twelve became minutes, I tried to prepare myself for disappointment. Obviously, they would tell the successful person first and get around to the losers later…

The phone rang. I held my breath, my heart pounding in my chest...

'Mrs. Bennett? Viv? It's Martin… Congratulations! You have just become a land-owner!'

21. Tanglewood Times

My very first purchase was a machete. Before I could trust goats in there, I was going to need a new stock fence all the way around. With a very steep drop to the railway bed at the bottom, the southern boundary traced the old railway line that was once so important to the market gardeners in the area. I didn't want the goats getting down there even though it was no longer used. I would also need a proper entrance gate, one wide enough to make the turn in from the single-track road with a trailer on the back. I would also need hardstanding for parking, and wood to make the tin shed habitable. I could do without electricity for now, but I would need to think seriously about a temporary water supply until I could get mains water sorted. Lots of jobs on my to-do list, and I attacked them with the zeal of a determined me.

My children and their friends rallied. A friend of Stephen's, a farmer's son from the village and keen to earn a few extra pounds, came with his tractor and post banger and knocked in the fence posts. Followed behind by Tam and ably assisted by Stephen and Alan, who tensioned the stock netting and wire onto stout posts as best as they could with a claw hammer; a trick I had learned during my riding school days. Not the best tool for the job, but it got it done. I set to work on the shed, making partitions inside, waterproofing the corrugated iron roof with a sheet of tough blue plastic, and making opening windows out of Perspex. I found a second-hand water bowser that I could fill up at home and tow down, and had countless tonnage of hardcore delivered which was raked level for the new parking area. Soon, it was ready for goats.

The goats that I had mentally picked out from Debbie and Roland's herd would not be any good to me in Devon. It was just too far away to make transporting them practical, but also because they had not been disbudded by a vet as kids. This meant that they had horns, and horned goats in the show ring tended to be frowned upon. There is nothing in the rule book to prevent goats sporting horns from being exhibited, it was just one of those old show taboos.

   Ideally, I wanted goats of my old breeding, but I wasn't having much luck. I was able to track down some descendants of Tam's goat, Morganna, but found they too had horns. Cad's sister Caelia had vanished without a trace; at least, I knew where she had gone originally, but it turned out her owner had moved on, left some goats behind, and the new owners (a college) wouldn't check earmarks and were very reluctant to speak to me. The British Alpines were no better. Kelpie, my pride and joy, had died without leaving a daughter, thanks to the vet's mis diagnosis and her twin sister may or may not have been among the ones found dead by R.S.P.C.A. at the place that had seemed so promising at the time. Skippy, her half-sister was in a commercial herd upcountry, and I was reluctant to move her… even if she was for sale, as I knew she was happy there from the Christmas card she sent me every year.

However, word got around, and it wasn't long before I was offered the pick of that year's crop of British Alpine kids from Ian in Okehampton. I liked the breeding, especially as on one side they went back to a friend's goat that I had a soft spot for, having looked after her for a while. I chose two, who quickly became known as Tiggy and Spot. One had a crumpled ear from where it had been chewed by her mother as a kid, but otherwise was very promising, and one who proceeded to spend most of the following show season in front of the kid that Ian had chosen to keep in the line-up. I also succumbed to the purchase of a young British Alpine male, Nightshaze Simon, bred by a good friend of mine.

Janet Brown in Portsmouth, whom I had got to know well following the purchase of Ivanhoe, Cad's sire, let me have a seemingly barren English goat of the type that she knew I liked, in the hope that a miracle might happen and she would produce a kid for me. So, I had goats again. British Alpines and English. I can't describe how good that felt.

Tanglewood was a great place to be. We had family parties down there, the grandchildren climbed trees and many a cup of tea was brewed in a little caravan that I bought to use as a shepherd's hut. Roland sold me a proper Ifor Williams sheep trailer, which he dropped off after delivering some animals nearby. I had never had a proper trailer before. Always a make do, so I felt like I had truly arrived. Owning my own land made me feel safe. I knew that the insecurities of renting and the mishaps of the past because of it could not happen again. I couldn't be kicked off my own land.

The man at the planning office had raised both eyebrows at the goat mansion, complete with shower and hot running water that I had designed. With such apparent luxuries, I don't think he believed me that it was just for goats; he had obviously never met a goat showing fanatic before who, after years of breaking her back and creating quagmires, needed facilities with proper drainage to bath goats in comfort, and everything to hand under one roof. My plans for this perfect goat set-up were denied as a result. My compromise was some brand-new field shelters. They arrived in kit form and were swiftly erected by Robin and Tam. They boasted a sensor light powered by a solar panel, by way of mod cons, installed by Robin but bathing the goats would be the old-fashioned way still, tied up outside with buckets of water.

I singled out and protected the trees with chicken wire that I wanted to save from the marauding goats nibbling, and between the goats and the rest of us, we thinned the rest.

Once the light could get through, young grass peeped upwards and, in the spring, the whole place erupted with daffodils and narcissi. It was a truly magical place. I had not been that happy for many years.

Converting the tangle of trees and brambles into a working goat paddock was a real family effort, helping to draw us together again after the shock of Mum's death. The twice-daily walks down the quiet little lane, lined by Devon banks that erupted with the pinks of the campions and foxgloves, after the whites, yellows and golds of the snowdrops, daffodils and primroses, not only helped to keep me and Woody the Spaniel fit but also helped my confidence at being out on my own.

I might have been the only human down there, but I did have the goats and Woody for company. Whilst Woody kept a respectful distance from the big goats, he liked to hold the kid's bottles for them when I needed another hand and would carry the empties home again. Once off duty, he would conduct a tour of the premises, marking strategic points to deter intruders in the best way he knew how. He could still make me jump when he appeared from nowhere, tongue lolling, happy-faced, back from his errands, always so silent on his fluffy, web-toed paddy-paws.

The concern that someone could be following me, waiting behind trees, or lurking in my hay shed, that fear of the silence that my poor hearing couldn't penetrate, was gradually replaced by a celebration of the solitude. I developed an appreciation of the way darkness changed from absolute, where it didn't make any difference if your eyes were open or closed, to the ethereal silver of a full moon where grasses shiver, touched by the wand of the evening breeze. Being so close to nature, especially mulling over my thoughts whilst milking in the semi-darkness, gave me an enhanced perspective of my place on this planet. I might put up fences, clear trees, and plant fruit bushes, but nature was only allowing me to borrow the land they grew on for a little while. Nature was patient, and She could take it back when I had gone. And the stars. On a clear frosty night, the sky was filled with them, tiny wee specs of glitter from millions of light-years away in a galaxy so vast, so awesome, that I couldn't begin to understand its complexity.

One night walking home, my thoughts off on some tack of their own, my attention was quite abruptly drawn to the skies. The stars that make up the sign of The Plough, or Great Bear, were massive and directly over my house. I know that the constellations appear in different places according to the time of year, but this seemed so obviously intended that I should notice, that it made me stop and just stare for a while. Was it Mum? Was she giving me a big thumbs up? I hoped so.

22. Edwardian Farm Fame

One of the more glamorous aspects of working at a visitor attraction was meeting the occasional famous person. I'm not much of a celebrity watcher and so there were probably a lot more passing through than I noticed. I certainly spoke with one or two over the years, including Timothy Spall, a long-haired character with an impatient manner that I was sure I recognised as Ian Gilmore, and Fiona Bruce and the Antiques Roadshow team when they came for the day when Morwellham was the host for their program.

Fiona was just as lovely as she appears on screen, and I even got to be on T.V. The sharp-eyed might just catch sight of me sweeping out of 'Quay Cottage' having just waved goodbye to my fictitious husband. My few seconds of fame compiled from hours and hours of filming us all going about our invented Victorian daily duties that day.

Most of my family were drafted in to act as volunteer Car Park stewards, and the shop volunteers (in a Victorian costume of course) walked up and down the lines of hopefuls hawking sandwiches and drinks from woven baskets like something out of Oliver… *'who will buy these wonderful sarnies.'*

But the real highlight for me during my time at Morwellham was the arrival of Alex Langlands, Peter Ginn, and Ruth Goodman, along with the Lion television crew. Morwellham Quay was chosen as the venue to film the historical documentary series 'Edwardian Farm', which aired on BBC 2 in 2009.

Meanderings of a Serial Goat Keeper

Ahead of their arrival, one of the writers, Giulia Clark, came to see me in the shop… she'd heard that I was something of a goat expert.

As well as handing over all my books on 'A hundred and one things to do with goats' milk' she also wanted me to source some authentic-looking goats that could be kept up at Morwellham's old farm, for the duration of the filming. This was not as easy as it sounds. Whilst English goats were the obvious choice, there were not as many around as there had been when I was first involved with them back in the 1990s. Moreover, no one really wanted to lend out their precious stock, even if it was for the chance of fame. However, with some arm-bending, English Goat Breeders Association members and husband and wife team, Annette and Paul, eventually relented. They made the trip from Buckinghamshire one afternoon, complete with a large adult male goat, a milker, and a kid.

Peter Ginn asked the most questions about them and demonstrated he had listened to previous instruction in the ways of animals, by asking if they should be tied to a loop of something relatively easy to break, in the event of them panicking. Something I would say more suited to horses than goats, but he impressed me nevertheless and was much easier to talk to than Alex. I never got to meet Ruth.

I don't expect that Meg, the farm manager was thrilled to see the goats arrive, as there had been goats at Morwellham before, the last being a canny old lady named Flo. Flo was marked like an English goat, but no one really knew much about her history. She was the queen of the farmyard and knew all the escape routes; 'Florence Alert!' was a frequent cry over the team radios during the summer months, when visitors needed rescuing from her picnic basket raids. Things

Edwardian Farm Fame

reached a peak whilst we had a temporary new farm manager, who solved the 'Flo issue' by tethering her down on the quayside, just out of view from the shop door. After the fatal incident in which Genny had had her shoulder broken, I spent so much time trying to keep an eye to ensure that she wasn't being taunted by school children, or barked at by visitors' dogs, that I convinced management that she would be happier somewhere else where she could roam free, in the company of her own kind, and she was consequently rehomed.

Sadly, by the time the filming started, the revenue generated from it was too late to save the struggling Morwellham Quay as a visitor attraction. Most of the staff had been made redundant, including me, before filming started, and by now it had gone into administration. As I was no longer working at Morwellham, I didn't have a lot more to do with the illustrious celebrities after their arrival, apart from the occasional phone call.

'How do we know when she's ready for the billy?' then followed by, 'How do we know if she's in kid?' But at least Giulia returned my books, along with a thank you note.

The goats didn't feature widely in the series. Viewers only got a fleeting glimpse of them in one episode. It seems they were more trouble than their screen footage was worth, and they were packed off home early. I hope Peter, Alex and Ruth were not too traumatised by whatever antics the 'capricious by nature' goats got up to that got them sent off-set in disgrace!

23. All Good Things…

Morwellham Quay went into administration in 2009, following the withdrawal of financial support from the council. We had known the end was coming for a year or two, and there had been many last-ditch efforts to save it.

Its heyday as a visitor attraction was around the mid-1980s. A time when I remember seeing adverts on the television for it as a Living History Museum, depicting throngs of happy visitors and lots of Victorian-costumed staff twirling parasols, rolling casks around, or tipping their stovepipe hats to the ladies as they strolled by. The novelty of a trip down the George and Charlotte copper mine, with 'Rick the Pick', drew the crowds and holidaymakers like goats to a rose bush. The vision for the interpretation of the site relied on oodles of staff, who took their designated character roles very seriously. Care to create costumes as authentically as possible, right down to the split-leg knickerbockers and the tie-on pockets that we ladies had to wear hidden beneath numerous underskirts and petticoats, our camisole, and of course, the essential crinoline.

The emphasis was on 'living history', in other words, mingling with the visitors, giving talks and demonstrations, interacting with the public rather than making them read information boards; but by the time I started working there, budgets were already tight and getting tighter, and there was only a skeleton staff to work all the roles. I was often pulled from the shop to give a talk as no one else was available, and if anyone

All Good Things...

left, they were unlikely to be replaced. Then the redundancies started. Mostly the longer term and higher-paid staff to start with, who were then replaced by casual seasonal staff to cover the tourist season and finally volunteers. Morale really plummeted when the stalwarts were asked to leave.

There were still coach loads of school children who visited to bring their curriculum lessons on the Victorians to life, but public visitor numbers had dropped off dramatically. Those of us who remained did our best. We loved the place with a passion and hated what was happening to it.

That last year, we had a new site manager. He was brought in from the council to try and turn it around. More staff were laid off, the farm closed to visitors, and what money was available was spent on the Ship Inn instead. The idea was to create a gastropub, that would draw people to the attraction. Peter Gorton, a local 'celebrity chef' popped down to oversee the arrangements. But the visitors didn't want fancy-fare; what they really wanted during the day was a pasty or chips, and it rarely opened in the evening. New parking charges drove the local dogwalkers away, with further revenue lost from the coffee or pasty they would have bought at the Ship, or a bag of sweets from me at the shop.

Too late, the call had gone out for volunteers. There were not enough, and of the ones we did get, few stayed. With no staff to interpret the site, little signage, and no guidebooks left to buy, visitors wandered about with no idea what they were looking at. I had to field a stream of complaints that there were no longer the cart rides with old Jack the Scottish Clydesdale that they remembered from their childhoods, and had brought their own children back to see... I missed him too. He would always have an aniseed ball from my shop at the end of his shift, waiting until he was given one before he would head up the hill to the farm.

We all contributed what skills and ideas we could to bring in some extra money. Some staff made up flower posies to sell. I found a stock of unsold old horseshoes I'd decorated some years before in my canal boat painting phase. Later, we made Christmas wreaths of holly, ivy, and sticks of cinnamon, and we roasted chestnuts in a brazier made functional by the site blacksmith. With the money we raised, we bought our bestselling lines of old-fashioned sweets. I am proud to say that the shop took more money than we spent, but it was not enough to hold back the tide and stop us drowning.

The shop became a popular place for staff to call in for cheering up between talks, but it was emotionally draining being the 'chin-up' person for everyone else.

It was a hard depressing time, there was no money for orders, anything on sale or return went back, including Rocky Rocking Horse. Seeing him loaded into the van made the dire situation so real and it made me cry. I really knew it was the end. Not long after, one dismal winters afternoon, I wound the shop clock for the last time, hung up my crinoline, and handed over the bunch of keys from my chatelaine. Our best had just not been good enough to save it.

The closure of Morwellham presented me with a problem. It had always between difficult to manage on a seasonal contract, but I had always scraped through somehow. Now I had no income at all. If my land had been attached to my house, I could have claimed

All Good Things...

benefits until I found another way, but ironically, because I was too poor to afford that option and the land was separate, the government decreed that it must be sold, and they would not pay me a penny until the money raised from the sale was all gone. I needed a job fast, or I would lose my goats again. So much for owning the land giving me security.

Finding another job was proving difficult. Over the last years, my hearing had deteriorated considerably. There was no way I would be able to return to the youth work I had been doing during my early degree years, where 'hearing' young people was a vital part of the work. It often took a lot of confidence for them to disclose an issue, so requiring them to repeat themselves was not going to happen. Anything involving phones, noisy working environments, machinery, or gadgets - like coffee machines, humming fridges or air conditioning fans, where I needed to hear speech, was impossible.

A temporary solution was to go back to finish the degree I'd interrupted to take care of Mum. I only had two semesters left to complete, and I remembered Dad's pride that I had gone back into education. It seemed like the right thing to do; it bought me time *and* did give me access to a grant of sorts.

I also took in a lodger. A talented violinist who had played for the popular local band, Mad Dog McCrea, along with his black and white cat, Casper. His rent just about made up for the invasion of my privacy and he proved helpful with the goats; especially once I found myself some work on the check-outs at Safeway (now Morrison's).

But the field and the goats that had been such a joy, now became my biggest anxiety.

My head was not functioning properly. The money worries, on the back of all the emotion that had gone into the death-throws of Morwellham, seemed to have impaired my cognitive ability. I really struggled to finish those last two semesters, complete my final assignments, learn the new job, and hold everything together... I succumbed to the doctor's suggestion of anti-depressants, so popular at the time. Abby persuaded me not to give up on the degree, helping me get through it. Even with her help, I barely managed to scrape a pass mark for those last two pieces of work. Thankfully, my previous grades were good enough to carry me through, and I still managed to graduate with a 2:1 honours degree.

I had further setbacks. A worried Abby came to find me one afternoon after I had phoned her on my way home from college; I don't remember but apparently, I wasn't making any sense. She found me upstairs on the bed. I'd put soothing music on, and made sweet tea, aware that I was in some sort of shock. The shaking and crying had stopped by the time she got there, but I was unaware of time and in some sort of faraway place.

Earlier that morning, for some reason, I'd challenged Paul, the relationship that had floundered on Mum's death, about a rumour I had heard about an affair he'd had while still with me. He seemed happy to admit to it.

It shouldn't have affected me as much as it did, we were no longer together and it was history, but my inner self clearly did mind very much. Although I had gone off to college as normal, apparently fine, it hit me later

All Good Things...

like a tidal wave. With the hurt came tumbling everything else. I had cried for the world. For every suffering child and animal, for anyone who had suffered loss, or was hurting as I was, I cried. I was struggling to shut the lid on the emotion box in my head.

Not long after that, I wrote off my car - just yards from home. The anti-depressants, along with the low afternoon sun, had made me sleepy. I had fallen asleep at the wheel, driving straight on, when I should have avoided the bank that projected into the road, and rolled my car onto its roof. Abby, unbeknown to me, and quite by chance, was following behind. She phoned Stephen at home, who pottered around the corner with a cup of tea. There really is some truth in what they say about being more likely to have an accident nearer home.

Fortunately, the only damage to me was laddered tights and a cut knee sustained from crawling out through the glass from the shattered windows, and the memory of Abby's panicked, 'For fuck's sake, Mum!'

Looking back, I was clearly not well, although I thought I was coping at the time. I had a string of unsuitable relationships, losing the younger children when I packed up the goats and decided to move in with a farmer in the New Forest; the boys, on the brink of GCSEs, moved in with their dad, and Elsie, just about to start secondary school, moved in with Abby. The madness continued, until one morning, when I saw myself in lucid clarity... and felt horribly ashamed.

It was Tam that I called. I poured my despair and shame down the phone, not knowing what to do or how to get myself out of the mess I had got myself into.

Meanderings of a Serial Goat Keeper

'Come home, Mum. Just put the goats in the trailer and come home... do it right now.'

I slept on her settee that night. Grateful not to be judged as I judged myself, feeling I had no right to any sort of loyalty from my children at all.

I'd given up my job at Safeway and evicted my lodger. I had no income and no savings. The insurance paid up for the wrecked Subaru, which tided me over for a while... but I had to face the facts. I would have to sell the field and with it my goats, unless some sort of miracle happened.

I thought my prayers had been answered when galloping over the horizon, in his trusty Volvo, came Mr Fisher. He was full of charm, seemed genuine, and what's more, had a chain saw... which was very handy for the bigger trees that needed clearing down at the field. Keen to impress me, he 'modernised' my kitchen and settled some of my outstanding bills. It was like something from a romantic novel. But turn the pages, dear reader, for all was not as it seemed: what happened next could have come straight from the blurb printed on the back of a dark romance novel, without the happy ending.

'Viv, down on her luck and reeling from a string of unhappy events, thinks she is saved when Mr Fisher knocks at her door. She is touched by the kindness and flattered by the compliments, given by a timely stranger who promises to save her. At first, she is unaware of his tricks - the gradual disposal of anything that is hers, or the insidious tapping of the wedge that separates her from her family. He convinces her to sell her house, her

All Good Things…

land, and rehome her beloved goats. With little to contribute himself, he persuades her to use her capital to buy a guest house in Torquay. But once the ring is on her finger, the dark moods her friends warned her about show themselves with no abash. He controls her food, her time, and her money. His rage frightens her. A cruel expression now contorts his once kind face. Realising her tragic mistake, she secretly plots her escape…'

Which is how both marriage, and goat keeping attempt number three, floundered.

Escaping the narcissistic, abuse in Torquay, covertly aided by my son Robin and his partner, I now found myself in a rented flat in Liskeard. I had an income of sorts, teaching lip reading to deafened adults; a qualification I had gained while at the guest house, under the guise of a way to keep the money coming in over the quieter winter months.

Then began the protracted, painful, and costly divorce proceedings from a bitter, vengeful, and abusive man. Never had I felt more like running away to the Hebrides. The solicitor was not optimistic. Fisher was not going to give up anything without a fight - not even the watercolour paintings painted by my Mum. It was ten years since Mum had died. It was her dying belief that the money she'd left me would make my life easier. Instead, I had lost everything but a tenuous hold on my self-respect.

24. Artificial Insemination

I don't think there was a female present that didn't wince as our male, fellow trainee pushed the bespoke speculum into the goat's vagina. It was quite a bulky affair that opened up like a duck's bill to enable him to peer deep inside, to locate the cervix through which, in theory, the straw containing goat semen could be inserted and ejected, hopefully leading to a pregnancy. The straw, until recently, had been kept frozen in a tank of liquid nitrogen but should now be nicely warmed, having been tucked inside the man's shirt for a few minutes. The poor goat didn't have much of a say in the matter as her head was between the assistant's knees, and her hind legs, tightly gripped at the hocks, were off the ground pulled tightly into the handler's chest. Something akin to the gynaecological stirrups that women must endure for various procedures, and just as undignified. It had been explained that the goat was fine like this for a few moments but after the trainee had been jabbing ineffectually to poke the straw through the cervix, he announced that he wasn't having any luck. The goat too had clearly had enough as she sank to her knees in a heap.

'Perhaps this is a good time to take a break?' suggested our instructor.

This course was one of my money-making ideas conceived during the Milton Abbot years, thinking that perhaps a family goat A.I. business might be the way to go. My thinking behind attending the course wasn't just to have a quirky answer to the question 'what do you do then?' should I ever be invited to a dinner party

Artificial Insemination

again. Artificial Insemination in goats was still a newish concept in the late 1990s and was yet to reach the same conception rates as with their bovine counterparts, but I could see there might be many advantages for its use. My thought that it could provide employment for myself and the family was genuine. I believed in its development, not just to have access to semen from males at the other end of the country, which was important to people like me with a minority breed of goat (males of the right calibre were proving hard to find), but especially as it should help to prevent the spread of diseases like Caprine Arthritis Encephalitis (CAE). CAE is a virus believed to have been brought to the UK by an infected goat imported from France and is contracted from bodily fluids in a similar way to AIDS in humans. Other diseases were becoming more common too, which was horrific to me, as goats had always been viewed as hardy disease resistant animals. Indeed, once-upon-a-time, farmers would run a goat or two with their cows, in the belief that they ward off Tuberculosis. But what is so frightening about CAE and its horrid friends is that many of them are slow, wasting diseases and therefore often not noticed until they have happily infected many others. If using AI was a way to help prevent the spread, then I was all for it.

Alas' I could see from Tam's face that my 'family firm' idea was not finding favour. Her nose wrinkled at the diagrams of the reproductive systems of both male and female goats' and she abstained from the demonstration on how the semen is collected. In this case a ripe little female goat was used to get the male in the mood and at the crucial moment an assistant swooped in to substitute an artificial goat's vagina for the real thing. It was all in the timing.

I have read that in some parts of the world a little electric shock is given to the male goat via the rectum which stimulates ejaculation, (how do they work these things out?) I may be wrong but I've not heard of this in the UK for goats as yet. The costs of setting up for business with the special tank for transporting the straws, even second hand, was disproportionately high, given the low conception rate. The handling of the dangerous liquid nitrogen scared me to death and the thought of a tank of it rattling around in the back of the van with the children was the stuff of nightmares. Neither, I realised, was I a free enough agent to set off to a needy goat with little notice. I had found the day fascinating, and both of us gained a licence to inseminate that lasted five years, but as a business opportunity it was not going to happen.

Tam still wrinkles her nose at anything to do with male goats, and A.I. for goats has never become as successful or as popular as with cows. It is still available, but it is more usual these days to use a laparoscopic technique done by a vet. Diseases, including one or two not seen before, are believed to be on the increase and sadly, despite the rigorous blood testing of the showing fraternity, positive tests for CAE as I write are now five in every thousand. I have seen reports that that herds on the continent now are riddled with disease. A vet working in Italy imported a shipment of kids and every single one tested positive for CAE. He sent them back. We are going backwards not forwards despite the advances in knowledge and technology. On a positive note, though, apparently

Artificial Insemination

goats are no longer tipped up like wheelbarrows for insemination.

25. Doesn't Get Much Worse Than This

Liskeard wasn't so bad, I decided, and my flat was better than it might have been. Two rooms had been knocked into one at some point, making the main room L-shaped, with windows on two aspects. I decided to put my bed at the top of the L in the main room, to save the one bedroom for any potential visitors. My lofty view was straight across to the blazing cross atop the fifteenth century church of St Martin, one of the three biggest churches in Cornwall. Below me and to my right, were the higgledy-piggledy rooftops that made up streets of the old market town.

There is still a livestock market in Liskeard, which is something of a rarity these days, but farmers shake their heads and mutter '*it's not what it used to be…*' It feels as though it's only a matter of time before this one is gone too. I have shown goats there in the past. The market was pressed into service as a venue for the Cornwall Male and Youngstock show, after Launceston Cattle Market, the original venue, was closed to make room for the town car park.

Nostalgia gave me a fondness for the limping-along market, and the old town of jumbled, mostly independent shops. More importantly, it had a rail station. This was important, as it enabled me to reach all five of the Lipreading classes I was teaching without having to rely on a car. My classes were all along the train routes, from Newton Abbot in Devon to Falmouth in Cornwall, carefully planned during my escape from Torbay in case a car was out of the question, as I had no idea what my finances would be.

Doesn't Get Much Worse Than This

My rented flat was also only a couple of miles from where Robin, his girlfriend Louise, and family were living. Louise and I joined the 'Slimming World' classes held at the church, and I was often invited around to their little cottage for Sunday lunch, to put back on some of the lost pounds.

I was getting my feet back underneath me, but it was slow progress. I was back on anti-depressants, prescribed by my sympathetic new G.P who felt I had a lot of unresolved grief I needed to acknowledge and then deal with. That was easier said than done.

The divorce was ongoing, and I had no idea what my options would be once it was finalised. I found that most unsettling.

One thing was clear though, I was unlikely to ever be able to afford to buy my own house again. Whilst I may have been able to find somewhere habitable on the Western Isles, I certainly couldn't afford anything in the Southwest of England. However, I wasn't sure if there would be much call for a deaf lip-reading teacher with a Somerset accent up there among the softly spoken Gaelic speakers. Besides, right now I needed the support of my children and friends and just wouldn't have been able to make that move alone. I resigned myself, again, to no more Hebrides or animals. Amid so much uncertainty, the flat was my sanctuary. Then, despite not looking, I met a farmer.

Will was everything that Mr Fisher had not been. He lived miles off the beaten track on Bodmin Moor. I got to play with sheep and help with the cattle. I walked the farm dogs and got taken sightseeing over the moor while squashed into the cab of the tractor. This was exactly what Viv's' liked doing. Most of all, Will was kind. After my last experience, I needed kind. Kind was now the highest ranking of my priorities, and anything else was a bonus. Will was looking for 'a woman'. He lived on his own with his daughter who currently did all the house-chores. She was about to move out and he needed a replacement. My pedigree, as the niece of Basil Young, known and respected by Will's family who happened to have been neighbours at one point, put me in the running as a contender. He upped the sales pitch. By an amazing coincidence, he'd always fancied a little place on the Western Isles. Maybe when he retired from farming...? My favourite breed of dog? Oh yes, he had always loved them too. What were Borzois like again? He would buy me one, two perhaps.

It seemed like he had fallen out of the sky like Mary Poppins and appeared to be everything I needed him to be. But experience had made me cautious. I wasn't sure about giving up the fragile hold on the life that I had just fought so hard for, to move in with him. When the lease to my flat was coming up for renewal, and his daughter's moving out date more imminent, he tried a new approach. One afternoon he said he had something to show me, a surprise... I had, of course, told him at great length about my goat obsession: the 'surprise' was an Ifor Williams P60 trailer. He could use it for the sheep of course, but wasn't it the sort that everyone used for goats? He had a barn he wasn't using, and a little paddock, sheltered by the farmhouse on one side and woodland on the other. He fancied having a few goats around but didn't know much about them. Could I help him? Which is how, despite my better judgement, I started in goats again, for the fourth time.

Although it had been a decade since the Tanglewood goats, I had kept in touch with the goat-keeping world and hearing my call, my friends rallied. Within weeks,

Doesn't Get Much Worse Than This

there were three English goatlings pulling hay from old style wooden racks, built above solid granite troughs. They were soon joined by a British Alpine male kid whose dam, Black Magic, I had coveted since I first saw her as a young goat at Devon County show one year. The fact that I was allowed to have this kid, when she had been promised to someone else was testament to the trust in me, earned from the old days.

He was perfect. He kept his breeder's prefix and the first part of his dam's name to show the lineage, but the rest was up to me. Born on a Sunday, Black Sabbath was the obvious choice.

He was only two weeks old when I fetched him, so I needed a supply of milk. I was offered a British Toggenburg milker, who was no longer needed in my friends' herd, along with a wether, (a castrated male kid), to keep Sabbath company. I had a herd again. I was a goat keeper again. My happiness was completed with the gift of two Borzoi puppies from Will. My family were happy too, at last they could stop worrying about 'Mother'.

'Mother' was happy sending off show entries and finding ways to use up the surplus milk from the gallons that Lupin, the British Toggenburg, was producing each day. As the kids were gradually weaned, so increased the levels in the briming pailfuls carried proudly into the house twice a day. I bought an ice cream maker, as Will loved ice cream, to emphasise what an asset they were. When the tame lambs' milk powder ran out, I switched them to goats' milk. Will seemed impressed, never had he seen such fat lambs.

In May, I took the three English goatlings to their first show, chuffed to bits that the Show Secretary had given them their own breed class. Not surprisingly, they took first, second and third places, in the absence of any contenders, but the judge did place them in the order I would have. I still had my 'eye'. They looked grand, plump, and sleek from their bramble control duties during the day and the best grade feed I could find. I was very pleased with them, and I had great hopes for their future.

Males, as I have mentioned, have their own show. Sabbath was entered for the Devon Male and youngstock show later in the year. The way he was looking, I knew he would be a contender for Best Male Kid. He was growing into a superb beast. Word soon spread that I was back again, earning me a new nickname: The Serial Goat Keeper.

The months passed. I was still teaching lip-reading, but the classes gradually dwindled to just one for a variety of reasons. There were yet more funding cutbacks, and the new classes I'd hoped to develop nearer home didn't happen. Yet my lesson prep for one class still took as many hours of preparation as it had for all five classes. I needed another source of income and, being Cornwall, I was able to get a job cleaning holiday chalets. I was beginning to sense that something was wrong between Will and me. Despite doing the cleaning shifts, I was still doing what I could around the farm. I was even getting somewhere with training the loony Huntaway pup that Will had bought for the sheep… but the moments we had shared faded. He no longer wanted me to go with him to the see to the further flung animals, and no longer talked about the goats with the same enthusiasm as before they had arrived.

Then I was the victim of dognapping and someone tried to steal my Borzoi puppies. I found Daisy, shivering by the back door, frightened and upset, but

Doesn't Get Much Worse Than This

her sister, Ghost was gone. Although we searched and searched every inch of the farm and surrounding moor, aptly named Ghost was never found. I was devastated. Even now, I still look on dog rehoming sites - hoping to find her. After that, Will became distant to the point of barely speaking to me. *Was it because of the missing puppy? Did he hold me responsible?*

Something wasn't right but he wouldn't talk about it, and I had no idea what I could have done that was so bad. Eventually it reached crisis point and I asked if he wanted me to leave. Sulking about something, he said he didn't know. I took that as a yes. My pride would never let me stay where I wasn't wanted, which meant the goats had to go and I was homeless again.

The English goats were easy to home. Sabbath, my stunning male kid, went on to win Best Male Kid at the Devon Male and Youngstock show, but with a friend, not me. Lupin, the milking goat who had done so well for us, had to go for slaughter. A promise I had made to her previous owners if I found I couldn't keep her. I had just not imagined it would be so soon.

I got there as early as possible, hoping to get through this awful thing quickly and with the least amount of stress to this sweet natured little goat. But with horrid irony, I had picked a bad time, getting there just as the slaughter men had gone off to have their breakfast. I stayed with her in the pen. A solitary goat and distraught keeper, among pens and pens of sheep. I hated myself for breaking the trust in me, and for letting this goat down. I vowed I would never again put myself in a position where someone else, on a whim, could decide that my goats were no longer welcome. It all happened so fast, and I had not seen it coming. It was a terrible, terrible time.

My remaining puppy, Daisy, and I moved in with Abby and her family in Exmouth. I no longer had the money for a deposit on a flat and renting with such a large pet was difficult. She was all I had, and I couldn't rehome her too.

Abby's house was already brimming with teenagers, so one extra body didn't make much difference, Abby assured me, even if it did mean usurping my grandson from his pit in the front room to a bed settee in the dining room. At night, only the kitchen and the bathroom were free from slumbering bodies.

I still drove the eighty miles each way to the clean the chalets at weekends for a while, until I found a job as a trainee Team Leader for a new Southern Co-op that was about to open. I had applied to be an assistant, not really wanting any responsibility at that time, but the manager needed Team Leaders and my C.V. showed that I had the capability. As it was an extra 20p an hour more and money was tight, I accepted the promotion with grace, despite my misgivings.

The divorce with Mr Fisher was still being dragged out, in every way he could drag it out. Everything seemed hard.

Fitting around my daughter's family was difficult at times. I lived out of the bag I had taken with me and tried to be as inconspicuous as possible; but it wasn't easy with a giant, fluff-shedding, six-month old puppy who had the ability to reach anything that took her fancy and a penchant for chewing things. I missed having my own things around me. I needed their familiar comfort.

Abby organised a convoy of her friends to go with me to collect my remaining belongings from the farm. I set

Doesn't Get Much Worse Than This

off first, to try and get it packed before they arrived, and stopped roughly half-way down to buy a strong coffee; I was beginning to feel a bit weird. I managed to get my van mostly packed, with my remaining things in heaps ready to load, by the time Abby's team arrived around lunch time. The A-Team consisted of my grandson Charlie with his car, and three others; the 'responsible adult' with Charlie as he hadn't yet passed his test, a good friend of Abby's fresh from a hernia operation, and Abby's then-partner with her camper.

I don't remember much of the day. I didn't seem to be capable of very much and was so glad to have their help. I felt very strange as we drove away. Tears were streaming down my face, and I had to concentrate very hard on my driving. Soul singer, Joe Bonamassa's *'Driving towards the Daylight'* gave me a strong beat to work to. I ate the cheese roll that had been pressed into my hands as we left in case my light-headedness was low blood sugar. But it made no difference; I didn't feel right. The light seemed very bright. I could only see what was straight ahead, and that seemed distorted, like I was looking through the wrong end of a telescope. I had to talk myself through each manoeuvre, *'...change down, increase speed again, change up. There's a speed limit, slow down, indicate left, pull into the garage, they said they need fuel...'*

I parked off to one side of the fuel pumps and made my way over to the others, distressed, and ready to apologise that I didn't have any money to pay for their diesel. As I spoke, I felt myself sway, and from somewhere distant I heard the hernia-op friend say, 'Catch her Charlie, she's going down!' I remember little else.

Meanderings of a Serial Goat Keeper

The iron strong box, containing the years of grief and trauma, had burst, and my head had shut down to protect me.

I was still clutching a soggy bar of chocolate when I was helped out of Charlie's car when we got back to Exmouth, which shows how seriously out of it I was. Under normal circumstances, no chocolate survives more than seconds once in my hand, and never has it lasted long enough to melt. It can't have been an easy journey for him having a semi-conscious grandmother, next to him in the passenger seat, for the journey home. Especially as from time to time I would semi come to and tell him to pull over as he wasn't supposed to be driving, before accepting his assurance that it was all fine and lapsing back to my previous comatose state. It was fortunate that we weren't stopped by the police as I think my capacity for the role of responsible adult was severely compromised. Somehow all the vehicles made it back, were unloaded into the storage facility and I was bundled onto my daughter's settee.

The doctor diagnosed 'temporary global amnesia'. Memory loss and confusion caused by prolonged stress, with the acute reaction of collapsing on a garage forecourt, triggered by the extreme distress of losing my goats once more. He promptly signed me off work for three months. The maximum he could allow me.

My new boss at the Southern Co-op wasn't pleased with this news. She had shown a marked indifference towards me since I proved to be a gentle 'green /blue' to her fiery management red in the silly '*Insight Tests*', showing that I much preferred to be an eagle on a lone mountain than a duck on the village pond. As I was still in the probation period, she took the opportunity to 'accept my resignation' as her letter put it. I don't really blame her; the new shop was due to open that week.

Doesn't Get Much Worse Than This

Will has since told me that his problem was the amount of time I spent with the goats. He assured me that he didn't *even* mind that I was deaf, he had got used to that and had never intended me to rear up and head off like a startled pony. He was just making a point. I wonder what part of *'Goats are my obsession'* he never quite grasped.

Meanderings of a Serial Goat Keeper

26. 2019 Moving On

'...Do you know the best way to load a stubborn pig?' Our driver half turned his head towards me as he delivered this question, startling me out of my daydreaming. I'd given up trying to join in the conversation from the back seat and instead, had been enjoying the world flashing past as we sped on our way to Bristol Airport. I was trying to quell the excitement gurgling about in my tummy, or perhaps it was the hasty breakfast of flask coffee and sugary snack biscuits Tam and I had shared in a lay-by earlier.

Five years had passed since the Will-the-farmer escapade. I had recovered after six months or so with Abby and a similar amount of time with Robin and his family. Scraping enough money from the divorce, I had managed to buy a government scheme house in Cornwall, and quietly got myself back on my feet. Resolute, I had spent the last two years studying for a master's degree in Creative Writing at Plymouth University. Today, Tam and I were off on an adventure. We were on our way to Stornoway, Isle of Lewis, Outer Hebrides.

Tam knows a lot about pigs. Her first job had been on a mixed farm with pigs. It had been an educational period of her life and many of her boss's expressions and expletives from that time have found their way permanently into the family vocabulary.

Our driver, 'Parkin' John', also knew a lot about pigs. Pig farming had been in his family for generations, before he discovered that looking after vehicles whilst

2019 Moving On

their owners were off on their holidays was a little easier and did a lot more for his wallet.

I sat forward; I'd reared a piglet or two on the surplus milk from my goats' years ago and could still remember the stress of trying to get them into a trailer. I needed to hear this. I could be about to find out where I had been going wrong. Besides, you never know when such a handy nugget of knowledge could be useful.

'Well now, pigs run backwards, you see? Point 'er arse towards the trailer, put a bucket on 'er head an' give the bottom of the bucket a good whack with a stick… 'Er 'll scuttle backwards into that trailer quicker un you can say hog's puddin''

The vision conjured by this explanation made it very difficult not to laugh and I had to concentrate hard on something else. Parkin' John seemed not to notice, and had casually moved onto the tale of how his father had lost his foot, accidently dipping it in the caustic tanks used for removing the bristle from the pig hides… Soon we pulled into the Airport and the conversation turned to more important things.

'Send me a text as soon as you land, and I'll pop back and pick you up. Monday evening wasn't it?' he added, checking the scrap of paper where he'd scribbled down the time I'd given him.

'Half past nine.' I confirmed with a nod.

I'd been writing about my goats as part of my Creative Writing course, which had led to a fishing-out of old photographs, and fond re-reads of Lillian Beckwith's books and a desire to see the islands once again. But the eventual decision to make the pilgrimage back had been prompted by the newsy update that had fallen out of Debbie and Roland's last Christmas card:

Meanderings of a Serial Goat Keeper

'Currently 11 dogs (all related), 22 hens, and three female goats, all related to Cad. (two twin sisters & 1 daughter). The daughter should kid in the Spring. No shortage of food & drink. You would be welcome, if you should think of coming to see us again.
Best wishes, Debbie and Roland

I'd asked Tam along because she had done the trip before and would ensure that we got there. She is organised and efficient, and doesn't suffer ditherers gladly, but despite that, we get on well and have many interests in common. I was confident that she would steer me to safety when I didn't catch tannoy warnings of bombs or similar, and she was also the only one available with a voice at a good frequency and pitch for my useless ears. Some may say 'loud'.

Bristol Airport was big, bright, noisy, and full of people hurrying to where they needed to be. We stood just inside the entrance doors, temporarily bemused, until Tam waylaid someone in a uniform to ask for direction. I trotted along behind like the dutiful parent that I am.

The anxiety of not knowing which queue we needed to join dispelled, we headed for the 'Ladies' followed by a forage for a second breakfast. We settled on a Boots meal-deal to share and took it off to a group of empty seats. There we made camp, heaving our rucksacks from our shoulders, and parking our small, wheeled suitcases in front of us to double up as tables.

Next to us was a suspended illuminated advert. It covered the height of the two floors and played a repetitive irritating jingle. Which, we realised, was clearly why the seats were free when everywhere else was standing room only. We looked at each other

2019 Moving On

asking the silent question, then shrugged. Could be worse, we agreed. Tam offered me an egg and cress, while we stretched out our legs and made ourselves comfortable. The departures board showed that our flight was delayed by an hour, so we had plenty of time.

After we'd listened to a rendition or two, munching in silence, Tam interrupted.

'What time were we *supposed* to get to Stornoway?' I felt in my pocket for my phone to consult the itinerary: but a bit like the picnic on our last trip, it just wasn't there, no matter how frantically I checked all my pockets, my suitcase, there was nothing, not a speck of a phone to be found anywhere. I was distraught. It was a brand-new phone, bought only two weeks before, replacing my old one which had relinquished its feeble hold on life at such an inopportune moment. I couldn't afford another new phone.

'I must have left it in the loo...' I wailed, pathetically.

'Wait there!' Said Tam with reassuring authority.

I watched in admiration at the woman my child had become. She cleaved her way through the heaving masses of the airport like a three-masted barquentine in a stormy sea. Neither of us is diminutive; a six-foot Tam in full sail is an awesome sight, reminding me of a similar time when Robin elbowed his way through the crowds when we had lost six-year-old Elsie at Devon County Show one year.

So, I waited, and comforted myself by telling my woes to the girl wiping the counter of the coffee bar next to our seats. She looked bored and had been listlessly wiping the same bit of woodwork for some minutes.

'People lose their phones all the time' she told me, before suddenly remembering a very important task that took her to the far end of the counter, and out of our conversation range.

The jingle started its round again as I sat waiting, alone with my thoughts, and my secret. In my bag, guiltily stashed between paperwork for the trip, were some estate agent's details. They were for a little croft-house on the edge of The Minch, that I'd made an appointment to view while we were there.

I didn't know what I was thinking of really. It would take every penny I had, leaving nothing for all the work the home report suggested it needed. I hoped they were more like guidelines than necessaries and argued with the devil on my shoulder that the work was mostly cosmetic. The previous occupant had done a lot to it when he bought it nearly fifty years ago, including a new roof.

'*If the shell is sound*', the devil on my shoulder whispered seductively, '*who cares about a bit of damp and the odd wood beetle? You've lived in a lot worse.*'

Access to the house was going to be a challenge. It could only be reached by boat, or on foot, along a rough track three quarters of a mile long over open heathland, for which, the estate agent warned, stout footwear was essential. Ridiculously, its inaccessibility was part of its attraction to me. I was in a rebellious mood. My time on this earth was ticking on, and I could see the years ahead empty with nothing-ness. I wanted one last adventure, to test myself. But I wasn't blind to the difficulties.

The remoteness of both the Islands and the croft, that made them so attractive to me, was also their biggest disadvantages. Unresolved questions, like: would the children be able to get there to visit? What if I broke a leg? How would I be able to get help or would I perish there cold and alone until the dogs ate me? And… what

2019 Moving On

about goats? What if it all fell apart again and they had to go?

Mum once said that there must be someone looking out for me because no matter what stupid things I do I always land on my feet. I've always tried to do the right thing, but what, I considered, if I was to knowingly do something that's a little bit daft, would whoever has had my back all these years finally wash their hands of me?

Perhaps it was too late for dreams. I have no room left for more scars on my conscience, or my heart... and now I had lost my phone.

I spotted Tam sauntering back across the walkway that joined each side of the mezzanine. She looks relaxed. Our thoughts met, and she gave me a thumbs up. Relief settles over me. Saved again.

Security at Bristol was much tighter than I remembered from our last trip, fifteen years previously. However, we negotiated the various stages of being patted down, X rayed, and processed, with only one slight mishap occurring when my shoe jammed the conveyor belt and Tam had to hold up her queue to come over and sort me out. Then there was a hasty repacking to get both backpacks and contents inside one case. Apparently, we couldn't have both, despite pointing out that a lady ahead of us had been waved through with her suitcase *and* a tote bag big enough to smuggle a St. Bernard. Fortunately, Tam was traveling light and had room for some of my essentials: she disputed the need for my complete set of Ordnance Survey maps for both Lewis and Harris, when we had two mobile phones between us. I retrieved them from the banished could-be-thrown-away pile and wedged them into my waterproof jacket's inside pockets, which gave me the appearance of someone wearing a bullet proof vest under their coat, or perhaps a vest loaded with explosives.

I don't know if it was the latter which made officialdom suspicious at Stornoway, but again I was called into a side room by two uniformed ladies. I couldn't hear what they were saying but nodded helpfully and behaved as indicated; stood lifting my arms, sat and lifted my legs, hoping that it was just bad luck that I had been singled out again and nothing that would require a full body search. Tam told me afterwards that they had asked my permission to be used for training purposes. Somewhat relieved my stashed maps had not singled me out as a suicide bomber, I decided I must just have that sort of face, but who cared! We were in Stornoway!

It was a dreary old February day when we landed, but I was back where I wanted to belong, with four days of stuff to do and a house to look at. We collected our hire car and set off for Calbost, via the Co-op as was becoming traditional for our visits.

27. First Day Away

We hadn't been able to give much thought to our surroundings on arrival the night before. It was dark, for a start, and we were tired from traveling, just pleased to have got there without getting lost. Our priority by that stage of such a long day was to get inside and put the kettle on. We found the door key swinging in the lock as promised, with a warm welcome waiting on the other side.

All the curtains had been pulled closed. A standard lamp cast its warmth over a tableful of goodies left for us; free range eggs from a croft up the road, Hebridean cookies, a bottle of wine a birthday card for Tam, which was a lovely personal touch, and a night's refund following Kiwi airline rearranging our flights, which I hadn't really expected but was delighted about. The ensuing muddle following their meddling, and not being able to hear when I tried to telephone to sort it out, meant that I ended up having to buy our tickets twice. I had followed their email complaint system but it must automatically self-destruct at some stage as I have never had a reply. So, this windfall was very welcome.

We drank our tea, ate the cookies, sorted out the heating, and gratefully called it a day before turning to our beds.

As soon as my body clock told me it was sunrise, I got up to draw back the curtains. I'm not one for lazing around in bed in the mornings, and usually sleep with the curtains open anyway, hating the claustrophobia of

Meanderings of a Serial Goat Keeper

being closed in and liking to keep to the rhythm of the seasons.

Although I know how stunning the Hebrides are, I was taken aback at the sheer beauty that greeted me that morning as I tip-toed out of bed and opened the curtains. It was not just its normal spectacular, but bathed in a such a peculiar vibrant light that it made me gasp, my breath catching in my throat loudly enough to bring Tam running, concerned that I was having some sort of fit. The Scots pines to the left of the window were sharp silhouettes against a timid sun, and the peaty waters of Loch Dubh in the valley below us were prickled with raindrops. To the west was the cause of the spectrum of light. Two full rainbows spanned the hills. I ran outside in my pyjamas and fluffy bed socks to get some photographs before it faded. *What a good omen to start our first day on the Western Isles,* I thought, thanking whoever was responsible.

A lone sheep skittered off with a flick of her tail and Goldfinches fussed about the pines. Looking down into the valley I could see the ruins of old blackhouses. Sad reminders of the times when villagers were forced from their homes to make way for large scale commercial sheep farming. The single-track road we had followed from the airport disappeared over the hills on its way to Harris. A few little white crofts dotted along its path, and I could see a fellow early riser unpacking a car in the distance.

Where else would anyone want to be? We had four whole days ahead of us. Tomorrow, although Tam didn't know it yet, we were going to view the house at Cluer. Then there were Harris Tweed exhibitions to visit… and the highlight of the week? We were invited to tea with Debbie and Roland, where I would meet Cad's great grandkids. I sighed a happy sigh; my now

First Day Away

soggy socks were stood once again on Hebridean soil. I snatched a last look at the rainbows overhead and went back indoors to change my wet socks. It was time for breakfast.

Feet dry and toasty warm again, we spent our first day catching up with ourselves and exploring our surroundings. We enjoyed a stroll, picking our way around the local ruins that are so typical of the landscape. Despite there being so many of them, it is impossible not to be affected by the silent tale told by these long-abandoned croft houses. They spoke of disrupted lives, of hardship, and of times when people mattered less than profit.

As if we found the pure gold at the end of the rainbow, we found more of their story later that morning in a folder discovered in a cupboard. It seems that our accommodation had once been the home of the late Angus Macleod, a local historian. He had documented every scrap of information he could find about the islands, especially this, his home area. In the house we were now sitting in whilst sipping our tea and finishing off the cookies, he had converted into a museum at one point in its history. We couldn't believe our luck.

Along with the folder of stories, there were local history society booklets and masses of other information. We spent the rest of the day reading through it all, reading out-loud to each other the bits that fascinated us the most, only looking up for food or more tea.

At some point during the afternoon, I had a light-bulb moment: this very house was the family home of Kenny Macleod, King of the Faeries! Of course, it was! Despite the plethora of Macleod's across the Islands,

Roland had said that Kenny had lived nearby and had waved an arm in this direction. I recognised some of the stories he'd told in the scraps of hand-typed documents. This made me happier than I can express. Our landlady later confirmed it; but delivered the affirmation with the sad news that Kenny had passed away a few years before. Thanks to Angus, our local knowledge had doubled, and our wish-to-see list was suddenly a lot longer; but that would have to wait. At the top of the list for the next morning, was the house viewing at Cluer that I hoped destiny had assigned to me.

28. Lost and Hopeless

The gate swung shut, with a self-satisfied *ker-chink*. It was a nice enough gate. But what it clearly wasn't, in its solitary, shiny, new, galvanised splendour, was one of two gates by a phone box. Which, according to the lady who had given us the key, would mean that we were in the vicinity of the house we were looking for.

I was getting to know this particular gate quite well, as this was the fourth time I had jumped out of the car to open and close it. I suspected that it had been put there by the owners of the grandly renovated house which stood beyond, dark and lifeless, inert and unresponsive to our knocking.

The 'key lady' had grown up on the croft next door to the house we sought; 'The Englishman's house' as she had described it, so her directions should have been spot on... but there *weren't* any other gates. My new friend here was the only one it seemed. The estate agent's bumf was no help either. Despairing and frustrated, I hurried back to the car, the increasing wind wrenching open the car door from my hands. The heater, warming the pages of the newspaper liberally strewn in the footwell to soak up the sodden puddle left by my walking boots, was giving off a fug of peaty moorland bog.

We drove back the way we had come, towards the road that would take us on to the Harris Tweed Clò Mòr Exhibition and the Shop in Tarbert, which was our 'official' destination for the day. Stopping off to look at the croft house, which just happened to be for sale, was supposed to be just idle curiosity on my part because it was so unique. But the prospect of a fifth unproductive trip up and down the road was pushing things beyond 'just satisfying idle curiosity'. I feared that I would soon have to confess to Tam that there was more to my interest than I was letting on, and I would have to admit that, ever since finding the advert, my imagination had been captured by the forlorn little house, and I had been fantasising about a new life there ever since.

The little croft had been on the market already about eighteen months, so I hoped the owners might be receptive to a slightly lower offer rather than put it through the ravages of another Hebridean winter. Clearly no one in their right mind would want it, so I felt I was in with a chance. The vast amount of work that needed doing passed over my head. If it was structurally sound, I reasoned, I would cope. After all, I had lived at Princetown with no proper heating. All that was irrelevant however, if we couldn't find it. I could feel my hopes dripping with the raindrops into the puddles at my feet.

It seemed like a good time to stop for our picnic to sooth fraying moods and decide what we did next. As Tam billowed about retrieving our lunch, which she had placed in the boot herself, to be certain of it, I fished the damp sales particulars from my pocket. Had I missed something? I wondered, checking it again; no, we *had* turned left at the signpost and we *had* followed the road to the top of the hill, but the promised 'For Sale' board that should be marking the start of the path to the house, just wasn't there - nor were the gates, or the phone box. I couldn't understand it. There weren't any other roads. Perhaps it had blown away, or maybe it had been appropriated to keep a few chickens from

Lost and Hopeless

escaping? Either way there should still have been some sort of evidence, one would have thought.

I chewed my way through my ham and coleslaw roll in silence, glad for a swig of tea to wash down the two-day old tiger rolls and stared glumly out of the side window to hide my despair. Tam had asked no questions when I'd casually dropped into the conversation over breakfast that we would need to get a wriggle on, as we had a croft viewing appointment on our way to the Harris Tweed exhibition. After just one long searching look, she had driven us forty miles in slashing rain and buffeting wind to see this cottage which didn't appear to want to see us; but there were limits to her forbearance of a parental whim. The sensible thing now would be to admit defeat and forget it. It was a stupid dream for someone of my age, alone, with little funds. What was I thinking of? but I had *really* wanted to be brave and have this last adventure.

The disappointment tightened and curled around my insides like a piece of baler twine tying a bale. Unusually for me, I was having a job to finish my roll.

The key to the house was still in the compartment by the gear lever where we had thrown it. It was a simple padlock sort of key, that really should have been under a flowerpot. Attached to it was a brown luggage label with the address written in tidy blue letters.

Surely', my head argued, *'where there is a key and an address, there must be a house?*

I thought back to another time we had been searching for a house on the Hebrides. That time, we had been fooled by looking for the obvious, literal, and ultimately, wrong thing. A misinterpretation of instructions. I wonder...?

'What did the key-lady say again?' Tam repeated back the instructions the ex-neighbour had given us.

'Through two gates up a hill with a phone box at the top.'

I tried to visualise the road as she spoke, traveling it in my mind... and then the penny dropped.

'Could it be that green B.T. junction box, back up there?'

Tam just stared at me with a disturbingly unreadable expression; we had been looking for a phone box of the traditional sort: large, and red, with a phone in it.

'Look... there's a gate post!' I exclaimed, pointing to some wire holding up what was left of a weather-eaten timber post. It had a friend across the road that also dangled forlornly. Both had clearly retired from holding up gates' years ago, but I was certain they had quite definitely been gate posts at some stage in their career. A little further on was a similar set. I cast my eyes further along the fence.

'Look there!' I yelled, forgetting Tam's acute hearing in my excitement, and waving my mug towards a barely noticeable gap in the fence about two feet wide, on the opposite side of the road to where we had been looking. Beyond was a faint track that disappeared away over the horizon. We had found it!

Tam muttered something that I didn't quite catch about proof of tenacity being part of the Hebridean test for new owners, and we hastily packed away our lunch. Tam was persuaded that she should wear my waterproof leggings, the only pair that we had between us. We knew from our weather apps that Storm Freya was making her presence felt back home in the South West, and although the weather was bad already, we also knew that she was currently just teasing us and was set to get much worse. Her full wrath was expected as the day drew on, and indeed was looking imminent, as swathes of grey were travelling towards us across the

Lost and Hopeless

waves of the Minch at alarming speed and the horizon was fast disappearing. We were going to get wet, but I felt prepared in a freshly waterproofed jacket, thick socks and walking boots, and clutched a compass in my pocket. I reckoned that I could cope with a bit of damp about my knees, so forfeiting the waterproofs to keep the driver happy seemed like a good strategy. I pulled rank for once, and Tam wore the trousers.

Off we trudged, following the path which wound its way around outcrops of gneiss and alongside a couple of small lochans. The hood of my jacket helped to lessen the effect of the wind blowing over the top of my hearing aids, but it still sounded like I had an army of sound techs in there blowing at microphones. Thus, communication was only possible with lots of pointing and exaggerated emoji faces.

Sometimes I was ahead while Tam took photographs. Sometimes it was me lagging behind and sometimes, where the path allowed, we plodded on companionably side by side until the sight of two little roofs appeared tucked away in the shelter of the other side of the hill we were currently climbing.

'There' I shouted, and I confess, broke into an unaccustomed sort of jog, I was that delighted.

As soon as I stepped over the threshold, I was gripped by a sense of calm that wrapped me in a hug of welcome. It felt warm too, and I wondered if that was because the thick walls were keeping the temperature ambient, as was found in caves and down the mine at Morwellham. There was a damp stain around the chimney breast, but no smell of mould. First impressions were favourable.

Meanderings of a Serial Goat Keeper

To the left of the entrance lobby, we could see into the kitchen, where an old stove was waiting for some black lead. Peeling lino, and Formica cupboard fronts, left open to air, sagged on their hinges. Looking beyond the recent neglect, the main room felt a cheerful room. It was easy to imagine a few dry peats burning in the fireplace getting the heart of it beating again; but the table, set with plates as if expecting someone for tea who never came, and the sideboard, with serving dishes and papers spilling out from the cupboards, felt lonely. It needed someone to love it again, and I could easily imagine myself eating creamy hot porridge here in the mornings. I could love it. I would love it.

It was hard to believe that it was no longer lived in, as it was looked as if we had broken into someone's house and they would come back at any moment, Tam commented as much. Especially poignant were a pair of men's brown leather shoes under the chair at the bottom of the stairs, coats still hung on the hooks inside the door, and an incongruous big-button phone sat importantly on a table by the bookcase. There were souvenirs of an interesting past-life everywhere. Carved trinket boxes, china ware and crystal cathedrals lined the shelves on the wall above the fireplace. Tumbled pebbles and sea-carved driftwood jostled with salt and pepper mills on the dresser. Book titles caught my eye. The Works of Oscar Wilde, The Looking Glass War, and Sir Winston Churchill, squashed in the shelves alongside Reader's Digest compendiums and several nature guides.

On top of the bookcase, I spotted a wedding photo. Was this 'The Englishman' with his bride? He did look typically English, in a simple-brown suit and she in flowing apricot chiffon that suited her dark skin. In the background were two girls dressed in the fashions of

Lost and Hopeless

the sixties. They didn't look as though they are wishing the happy couple well. Were the newly married couple warmly received here by the Islanders, I wondered? I could only guess at their story. I hoped they had found happiness when they moved to this little love nest nearly fifty years ago. I wished I could talk with them now.

The two bedrooms and the bathroom upstairs were accessed by a wide wooden staircase, which turned with a mini landing about halfway. There was a small window looking out to the rear of the house fastened with a bent nail and several coats of white gloss. It was not much use as ventilation, but even on such a stormy day as this it let in a surprising amount of light. Rubbing a patch clear on the grimy glass, I looked back over the way we had come. A few sheep were crossing the path in search of shelter as the weather was coming in, and I wondered what my dogs would make of them. I didn't trust them not to chase sheep. My thoughts now wondered how I would contain them in such an un-fenced area... staggering along that path, with a 30kg sack of goat food on my shoulder, wouldn't be much fun either. I said as much to Tam.

'Quad bike,' she said, 'or you get a dinghy with an outboard. You could get to Tarbert easily by boat. Then you'd only have to carry stuff up the garden'. Garden being a loose term for the clumps of rushes and rocks that sloped down to the water's edge at the front of the house. I was dubious about this. We were talking mechanical things now. I could possibly fool a complete novice with my talk of loose tappets, transverse engines, and popping core plugs, but probably the most important thing I knew about engines, is that they break down... frequently.

'You-Tube Mum. You've taught yourself how to do most things. Men do it, so how hard can it be?'

I said that I rather thought men do it because we are clever enough to let them, which made us both laugh; we carried on up the stairs, the anxious moment dissipated for now. I also realised that I could drop the 'just looking' act. My daughter knew me well enough, and I could tell that she was loving the place as much as I was.

It felt like a museum. I could imagine the owner of the shoes sitting at the writing desk of what was obviously his room, gazing out of the window where the sea foamed over rocks and the coloured pebbles of the shore, and seabirds screamed to the chorus of the shsssh of the waves. A writing tray held old fashioned fountain pens and a pot of liquid ink. I wondered if he was a writer too; it was a perfect room for inspiration and dreaming. I took the liberty of sitting in his chair to take in the view from the window. *No catch for the fishermen today*, I mused, watching the Minch getting angry. I wondered if there were any out there still, who had left it too late, wrestling now to keep their little vessels head-on to the swell? Safer to be at sea, riding out the storm, than risking the malevolent rocks of the coastline, while they waited for Freya's wrath to pass. Fishing is a hard way to earn a living…

'Mum…' Tam broke into my thoughts. 'MUM…! I said, we should be getting back, it's blowing a hoolie out there… Don't forget, it's quite a walk and we don't want to get lost in this sort of weather.'

I nodded, turning from the window to take a last look around the room. I wanted to remember it, to absorb some of the atmosphere to take home with me. She was right. We should go, but I didn't want to leave. I had to squash the thought I may never see it again. I knew that

Lost and Hopeless

a little piece of my heart would always live on in that room.

The wind was raging in from the sea as we negotiated the rocky land to the rear of the house and found our way back onto the path that took us to our abandoned little hire car. The sudden squalls made us totter forward a few steps every so often, as we struggled to keep our balance. But we were in good spirits, even stopping to make a French-and-Saunders-type video clip, our hair-whipped pink faces peeking out from tightly tied hoods, laughing as Tam narrates the absurdity of our escapade, and I get blown sideways off-camera. We were able to squeeze another cup from the flask when we reached the car. I spread a plastic carrier bag over my seat to protect it; I was a lot more than a little damp around the knees. The condensation quickly sealed us from the outside world as the tiny car rocked with the buffeting of Storm Freya's gusty breath... and I loved it.

'No one can say that I don't know what it's like here in bad weather,' I comment eventually.

'It must be awesome in the summer,' adds Tam, 'with the sea lapping at the bottom of the garden like that.'

Which brought the words of Miss Peckwitt's landlady, Morag McDugon to mind. Taken from her second letter to her proposed new tenant in *The Hills is Lonely*:

'Surely it's that quiet here that even the sheeps themselves on the hills is lonely and as to the sea it's that near that I use it myself every day for the refusals.'

Which reminded me of more practical matters.

'Did you notice that waste pipe that just stuck out of the wall and didn't appear to go anywhere?'
'No,' said Tam. 'Tweed exhibition next then?'

29. 'From the Land Comes the Cloth'

The men loading an old van onto the bed of a lorry in the nearby village gave us an amused wave as we drove past. We had asked them for directions earlier in the day when we'd been looking for the key lady's house. This time it was my fault we were going the wrong way. I'd insisted on a left turn when it should have been right, or the other way around. Navigation has never been a strong point, and usually such responsibilities were removed from me. Where was Alan, my navigation expert, when we needed him?

We hoped the men would have finished loading and gone by the time we sneaked back yet again but no, there they still there and enjoying a tea break. They all waved heartily as we tried to creep past unnoticed. No doubt, making scornful fun of hopeless tourists getting lost was a similar sport to them as enjoyed back home by the locals in Cornwall. There were other similarities I noticed to home; the *Gate in Constant use* and *No Parking Overnight* and *No Campervan* signs were all too depressingly familiar, something I had not noticed fifteen years ago on my last visit. The advent of Facebook has a lot to answer for. Those 'Best Kept Secret' images of stunning lonely stretches of white sand and startlingly blue seas were now shared widely, attracting a different sort of visitor to the ornithologists and botanists of the past.

We were on our way to the Clò Mòr Harris Tweed exhibition. I had emailed ahead from home expressing my interest and asking if it would be open out of season. The owner replied that it wasn't usually at that time of year, but on the day I mentioned they would be working there in the morning and would leave it open for us.

Sure enough, the door was open when we eventually got there. We knocked cautiously, feeling like interlopers, but soon engrossed ourselves in the exhibition. I was particularly impressed with a book on display, called *From the Land Comes the Cloth* by Ian Lawson. A book I would love to get my hands on, but it is a little out of my price range at well over a hundred pounds. The imagery of his photographs is startling. It visually demonstrated how the natural colours of the islands inspire the colours and cloth, and woven throughout its pages, and was written in an easy descriptive prose that I envy. Truly a work of art that takes you all over the islands, and despite its luxury price ticket, it is still cheaper and easier on the carbon footprint than the air fare for a visit.

Harris Tweed is remarkable for its durability. It is also a protected brand, like Cornish Pasties. To earn the orb trademark, awarded by the overseeing body, Harris Tweed Authority, the wool and finished cloth must be processed and woven on the Outer Hebrides. The rich colours are created from scoured fleece, which is dyed and then blended to exact recipes, before being spun into yarn ready for weaving. This is important to get even colour. If a weaver is deemed skilful enough, they can apply for work from the Authority, and the finished cloth would be collected from their homes. *How I would love to do this.* It is still a cottage industry that is very much thriving. Harris Tweed is very special, especially to someone who loves all things woolly, as I do. I still have two spinning wheels; Tam has an interest in historical costume, and we both adore fabrics. I was awestruck by it all, but particularly

'From the Land Comes the Cloth'

captivated by a scratchy black and white film of a woman spinning with a younger woman carding for her. Moments in time that could never be repeated, yet the wheel would have kept spinning and the girl's hands kept on brushing. Both sat by the back door of their turf-thatched croft house in the sunshine, until some task or other called them away. It takes me about an hour to spin an ounce of wool (twenty-five grams) and it would take about thirty-two of those to knit a mans jumper, depending on the thickness of the wool. A further forty to sixty hours to knit and make it up. It's no wonder that so many photographs of women from the pre-industrial age feature knitting needles seeming permanent in their hands, like mobile phones of today.

These island ladies worked so hard. Barefooted women smiling at the camera, bent almost double with creels of peats strapped to their backs. Women salting fish to store for the winter. Groups of women waulking the cloth, the finishing process for woollen cloth, and is known as 'fulling' in English. It was done by hand then, fists and fingers swollen from the punishment of beating wet cloth against the table for many hours. I stood, mesmerised by a grainy black and white film clip of a group of women seated around a table singing in Gaelic, waulking the sodden, newly woven cloth. Pounding their fists against the table with their section of the cloth, before passing it on to their neighbour in a continuous rhythmical round. I am completely in awe of these women. Beckwith writes how Miss Peckwitt teases her neighbours about an island man's preference for bigger women as their brides, with the reason given that the men believe that larger women have a greater capacity for hard work. Looking at these images, I can see why that would be considered important.

Meanderings of a Serial Goat Keeper

Having seen the exhibition, I was even more determined to equip myself with a Harris Tweed bag to take home, a secret desire I had been trying to squash ever since it had reared its little head. I could justify it to myself, as I did need a new one and what could be more fitting as a lasting memory of this time and place... but I couldn't really afford it. I hoped there might be a seconds-stand, and my chance might come that very afternoon: our next planned stop was the Harris Tweed Shop in Tarbert... assuming we could find it.

The displays inside the tweed shop had the immaculate look of a winter's afternoon, when everything has been dusted and tweaked, restocked, and priced, and there are no more odd jobs left to do, and all eyes are on the hands of the clock willing them to move faster. The two young girls at the till, made up as though they were out on a glittering night out in London, did smile as we blustered in out of the rain; but having worked in retail myself, I recognised the expression behind the movement of the lips. What they were really feeling was irritation that their chat had been disturbed by two scruffy tourists, just before closing, who would wander around the shop for ages, dripping everywhere, disturbing the displays, and then would leave without buying anything. Which is more or less what happened.

Despite a recording of a live Runrig gig wooing me, and the abundance of obvious attention to customer buying preferences training, there was very little in the shop that I could afford. Abby's request for a tweed collar for Nellie her Labrador, was out of the question at fifteen pounds; but I did hesitate at the bewildering array of bags, trying to decide which I would buy if only I could afford one, before Tam dragged me away.

'From the Land Comes the Cloth'

'Don't even *think* about it!' she told me eyeing the price tags. After much debate, we settled on a couple of Harris tweed fabric scraps attached to keyrings and some fabric squares masquerading as coasters to take back as souvenirs for the family. We thanked the girls politely as we paid, and they locked the door behind us to cash up.

That night, cold and wind battered, we dined on comfort food; 'Aunty Betty's roasties and Yorkshires, frozen veg and Fray Bentos pies followed by a real old favourite, Devon Ambrosia Creamed Rice, bought from the general stores in Tarbert. The Lifton factory where the rice pudding was made had been close to our house at Milton Abbot. It used to be possible to get hold of their 'seconds' very cheaply, sold as food for puppies' but there was nothing much wrong with it, usually nothing more serious than a mislabelling, no label at all or an over-caramelising. My children will not be the only ones in the region to have had their meals supplemented in this way and way too sweet for dogs.

My evening's entertainment was a copy of the Stornoway Gazette. I do enjoy a good local paper, as there is no better way to get a feel for the area it represents. The middle-class Tavistock Times for example, takes care not to offend with front page headlines and tell us that the daffodils generously donated to the town by Fairway Furniture were blooming nicely this year, or just occasionally, would allow a little outrage that the toilets in the car park were closed. In stark contrast, any ideas I'd had of leaving a paper out for the guests in Torquay were dashed by the weekly headlines of stabbings and drug raids.

Meanderings of a Serial Goat Keeper

It was possibly a slow week for the Stornoway Gazette. Its front-page headline of 'New Contract for Arnish on Horizon' did little to excite me, but it was a satisfyingly fat paper with interesting snippets and some quiz pages. I noted that Luskentyre beach, famous for its long stretches of lonely silvery white sand and romantic ponies of a similar colour, had won second again in the 'Best Beaches in the U.K.' awards as decided by Trip Advisor and I had a little chuckle at the name John Dory, (a type of fish) who was one of the columnists, before messing up the 'easy' Sudoku and failing horribly at the quick crossword. Time to put the paper down.

I felt happy as I nodded off to sleep later, remembering how impressed I was that the key-lady's husband had spotted us in the shop at Tarbert, and had said hello. It felt as though I belonged already. But as sleep finally claimed me, it was the long list of last names in the 'hatched, matched and despatched' section of the paper that made me smile, as I remembered Tam's irreverent comment that in the days of manual typesetting, the letter 'M' must have worn out much quicker than any other. Newspapers are a great source of personal entertainment.

30. Meeting the Kids

'I'D LIKE A CUP IF YOU'RE PUTTING THE KETTLE ON' came a yell from Tam's room; I'd forgotten that she had such acute hearing that she could hear spiders scratching against the walls. I thought I was being stealthy.

'Okay…' I sighed as I filled the kettle. I had woken early and had found it impossible to get back to sleep. It was either because I was excited at the prospect of the day ahead, or the freezing temperature.

Apparently, the electricity had gone off during the night. We assumed it was because of the strong winds that had buffeted the little house until the early hours; yet we were getting off lightly, according to the weather forecast. The tail end of Storm Freya had hit the South West much harder than the Islands, making Tam worry that our flight home would be cancelled; she was missing her children. But the world outside our little croft was still now, with that eerie quiet that happens sometimes after a storm.

It was Sunday and our last full day on the Hebrides. Tonight, however, not only were we invited to tea with Debbie and Roland, but we were also going to meet the goats.

We scoffed a quick bit of toast and went for a last explore of our immediate surroundings. From reading Angus Macleod's notes, we now knew that as many as five families had been trying to get by on the croft land that our feet currently trod, as late as the 1940s, with very little by way of help or facilities. To put this in perspective, at the time my parents married in the 1947, despite the aftermath of the war, they had enough to eat, and milk that came in bottles left on the doorstep, these hard-working crofting families, with barefooted children, were still having to leave their land. Their suffering and loss dismissed somehow, by the term 'depopulation of the Islands'. It was impossible not visualise the families sat around the peat fire in the blackened stones of the hearth, where perhaps water boiled or warmed the bones of the elderly. It felt disrespectful to enter the graves of their homes, and by some common understanding we stood awhile in silence, sad for the sufferings of the past.

We followed the sheep path down to the beach, where someone had recently piled stones to make cairns. I wondered if it was my fellow early riser. I stared out to sea watching the greys merge and swell, the thoughtful mood still with me, for a good few minutes before realising that we were being watched. A whiskery snout with large eyes regarded us just offshore. I grabbed Tam's arm and shook it to get her attention; as we looked, other smaller heads popped up. In all, at least half a dozen seals showed that they were as curious about us as we were about them. Seeing the seals made our morning and lightened the sombre mood that the ruins had evoked. We went back for a quick bite to eat with much happier hearts.

In the afternoon, we had planned to try and find the graves of two boys described by Angus in his folder of notes. There should be just about enough time before we were due at Debbie and Roland's. We wanted to pack in as much as we could while we were here; keeping busy would help the time pass too, as I was

Meeting the Kids

very excited about seeing the goats. Tam, perhaps, was less so.

It was the mystery of this story that piqued my curiosity of these two lads. Angus had estimated that the graves predate the middle of the 18th century, on the premise that the earliest known map of the area, dated 1760, already records the beach as having the name 'The Brother's Beach', or 'Mol Na Bràithrean' in the old Gaelic. Unless by some other coincidence it had been known as that all along, it would evidence that the two boys were found prior to that. It seems logical then, given that the custom was to bury people where they were found, to assume they had drowned and washed up on the sands; but who were they, and where were they from? If anything more had been ever known about the two boys, it is long forgotten now.

The graves were just clear of the shoreline marked only by a few stones apiece. One or two at the head end and again at the feet, but unless you knew what you were looking for you would have just walked right on by as they were well hidden, almost grown over with the sheep cropped grass, raw and irregular, not at all like the neat rows in a cemetery.

We were lucky to have found them, as we had almost given up looking, but Tam had left me taking a breather, sat on a rock watching the tumbling waters of a little tribute stream and musing again at the rainbow that was following us that day, and struck off over a sheep fence (we were careful not to do any damage). There was no brown tourist signpost, coffee shop or souvenir brochure to help her, just Angus's description.

After several minutes, I saw the red spec in the distance that was Tam, wave, so hurried over to join her - getting my feet very wet in the process. Seeing those stones was an awesome moment in the word's truest sense. We stood in silence for a while, thinking our own thoughts, and wondering about the boys and their families. We both realised that we could be some of the last people to see these stones, to know them for what they were, before they are grown over completely and lost.

We had planned to see the ancient standing stones at Callanish the following day on our way back to the airport, but every guidebook ever opened about the Western Isles talks about them. Here, we had just seen something *really* special. If not for the diligence of Angus Macleod and his love for his heritage, we would never have had this privilege.

The plan was to go straight on to Roland and Debbie after our jaunt, but I felt a quick sock change might be a good idea. By the time we got back to our little hideaway, the headache that had been threatening Tam all day, had developed into a headbanger. I made her a cup of tea, fished some paracetamol out of my pocket and left her comfy on the settee with the tv remote to hand if needed. I walked the half mile or so up the road, to where Cad's great grandchildren awaited me.

The last time I walked this stretch of road was fifteen years earlier, towards the end of my first visit in 2004 - to round up the escaped Galloway Gang, the rescued feral goats taken in by my friends. I looked up at the steep slopes that I had clambered up so easily that day, and marvelled that I had ever been that fit. The hills wore the browns of winter, forbidding and austere in the dusk. A contrast to the multi-shades and tones that summer's day, way back then. It gave me that strange feeling of familiarity, yet with it, a sad sense of distance in time. So much had happened since then.

Meeting the Kids

My timid first tap on the door went unheeded, so I readjusted the bottle of red wine I was in danger of dropping and tried again, knocking hard enough this time that the dogs heard. The wine had been part of our welcome gift from the landlady of our holiday cottage, but it was all I had to offer my hosts. I wished I had more to give, as they had done so much for me, and I hoped they would understand.

The garden and little path from the gate looked comfortingly familiar despite so many years having passed since I last saw it in the daylight. The craggy heap of Lewisian gneiss to the right that I had climbed daily to attract a signal to my phone was still there. And the little stream that Debbie and I had spent a happy hour or two unblocking, still busied on down to the lochan that still held a shimmering of silver from the darkening clouds.

But there was one new addition to the view that was hard to miss as it completely dominated everything. It looked to be an expensive build and, I imagined, very luxurious inside. It was a masterpiece of design, but nothing like the little croft houses dotted around about it.

My musings about planning regulations were interrupted by Roland's voice clearing a path through several dogs to the door, which opened allowing three or four assorted collies to push past him to encircle me and take turns at sneaky sniffs of my legs. The remaining pack continued to let everyone know that someone was at the door. Debbie appeared behind Roland and gestured for me to come on in, chivvying the remaining pack outside, to enable conversation.

We went through to the best room where I was shown to a throw-covered settee. We had mostly lived in the kitchen or the dining room when I had stayed before, so the immaculate room was unfamiliar to me. I had only been in there once when Debbie had been showing me how she was entering all the goats onto a database. This was cutting edge stuff at the time and I had been immensely impressed.

I proffered the bottle of wine to Roland who examined the label suspiciously, before suggesting that as the meal was almost ready there would not be enough time for it to breathe... so perhaps, something from the decanter?

Roland let the dogs in again while he went to check on the cottage pie; they seemed more kindly disposed towards me now that I was sat down, and several jumped up to join me. They were mostly the result of two unplanned litters. Suitable homes had not been forthcoming and so here they had stayed. The proud father of the youngsters was a large black and white working type collie of the sort that nudges your arm if you stop paying him attention. The rest skulked around with the occasional squabble over one of the many bowls of dog biscuits placed about the room. Roland kept order while Debbie told me stories about the goats.

Then the moment I had been waiting for; *'would I like to come and see them?'*

I followed Debbie, her packet of ginger biscuits, and bowl of vegetable peelings, across the yard to the goat shed. Several dogs followed, and I felt the occasional nip to my calves as dad-dog and his pups-in-training herded me along. The goats were tucked up in their pens, ready for their bedtime routine. Roland was sloshing in and out with water buckets, aided by more of the dogs. Debbie waved me into the shed with the air of a magician about to show you the best of her tricks.

Meeting the Kids

There they were. I breathed in; the heady smell of goat-shed took me right back to goats of my past. Although I had an awareness of the other goats in the shed, at that moment my attention was taken with the goat right in front of me. Her name was Madelynne, a black and white goat with two kids. She looked anxious about this stranger invading their home and circled in the straw, ears flicking to and fro, before taking up a position at the rear of her pen where she could watch me. I spoke quietly to her, wishing I could do more to put her at ease. She listened with obvious intelligence, but she wasn't ready to trust me just yet.

Debbie explained that Madelynne's sire had been bought in British Alpine who, I was delighted to learn, descended from a male goat that my Runrig loving friend Maggie and I had once driven hundreds of miles in a hired van to fetch. We shared him between our respective herds for a season in 1996. His name was Willamiss Cupid. A large rangy male with a genial temperament. Sue Gow's Alailah herd of British Alpine's, that I had admired so much, also featured in the ancestry, and more recently, British Alpines from Mrs Aitken's Rogerian herd.

On her mother's side Madelynne descended from Cad, and his fellow English goats. There were some Millwind goats there too, relatives of Cad's father, Ivanhoe. But Cad was there on both sides of her mother. He was her great-great-great grandfather on her grandmother's side and great-great-great-great grandfather on her grandfather's side. Madelynne might have been black and white like a British Alpine, but she had the look of Cad about her too. She was stunning. With so many illustrious goats in her pedigree, I was not surprised to learn that you could 'cut her milk with a knife' it was that rich. Madelynne was clearly the best of both breeds.

Her kids were charming, as all kids are, obligingly cavorting around the pen for me to admire. At the far end of the shed was Madelynne's twin sister, with her grown up daughter in the pen between them. All of them black and white. I was standing in a shed of beautiful goats that had all descended from one of mine. The work put into breeding Cad had not been lost. These goats may look more like British Alpines than English goats, but I loved both breeds and knew that the English gene would be there just below the surface and all the characteristics saved. These were remarkable goats, and I coveted them badly, but that night, as I plotted and schemed how to make my new life happen, those few little words from long ago wove through every thought:

'You will come home Mum, won't you?'

31. Coffee, Chips and Harris Tweed

I didn't want to go home. I wasn't ready. There was so much more I wanted to do. We had just parked in Stornoway outside the Harris Tweed Authority buildings, where we noted that for a small charge, we could have a look around their exhibition. As there was an hour or two before checking in at the airport, we decided to hunt down some coffee and come back to it. Our hasty trolly dash on arrival five days ago had not run to coffee, as tea is our usual beverage of choice. But after so many days' abstinence we were getting withdrawal symptoms. Stornoway is the main town on Lewis and home to around eight thousand people, about a third of a growing population on the archipelago. Home of both the airport and the harbour with the ferry link, it was a busy place. We were confident that we would find a steaming cup of freshly ground caffeine somewhere.

We were wet and cold, having been caught in a hailstorm at the Stones of Callanish, whose café (and toilets) had been closed; hence why finding a coffee shop of some sort took priority over the alure of a further tweed exhibition, and we set off to explore some likely looking streets.

I had hoped for a traditional little place where I could hear the soft lilt of the Hebrides one more time as an enduring memory to take home, but out of season, most places were closed. Surrounded by water both in the sea and falling on us, the urgency to find somewhere for our 'comfort break' increased. Tam was forging ahead, and so didn't notice me hesitate outside a shop that had a big SALE notice in a window that was displaying Harris Tweed bags. The sales assistant inside caught my eye. I pointed to the bags and gave an exaggerated sigh with a shrug of my shoulders. We exchanged grins, and I hurried on to catch up with my daughter. They were still more than I could afford, even in the sale.

Having not found our coffee (or loos) anywhere in the main street we branched right, striking lucky almost immediately: we spied a swinging sign portraying a brimming cup of frothy coffee. It was hung over what looked the door of someone's house, but it said OPEN and we were desperate. Pushing back the hoods of our waterproofs we tumbled inside to the jangle of a shop bell and found ourselves the only customers in a Chinese takeaway.

The two young men behind the counter seemed surprised to see us but gave us an enthusiastic welcome none-the-less. It wasn't exactly what we'd had in mind, but as we had already dripped over their floor it would have been rude to about turn, and coffee was coffee after all.

While Tam ordered, one of the lads spoke to me with a charming smile. I couldn't hear what he'd said so I looked at Tam, who was raising one eyebrow.

'HE SAID, ARE WE SISTERS?'

I added some chips to our order.

I wanted us to enjoy our last few hours on Hebridean soil, so kept my thoughts about the café décor to myself while we waited and took it in turns to make use of the facilities. I tried to concentrate instead on the comfortingly stodgy chips that I was imagining

Coffee, Chips and Harris Tweed

bubbling out the back for us, but the depressing grey and sage greens were hard to ignore. They lacked the sunlight needed to make them look smart and the oversized canvasses of a New York skyline, seemed so at odds with such a stunning remote island setting.

I was getting a headache, not helped by the clatter of the cutlery on the glass and chrome tabletops, which sent shockwaves searing through the amplification of my hearing aids. Perhaps the caffeine fix would help? The dull thump in my temples seemed to recede as I studied a poster behind the counter featuring a Barista's delight, so I was sure a cup of something like that would soon sort me out and I didn't want to worry Tam by resorting to paracetamol unless I had to.

I noticed that she was being unusually quiet. I followed her eyes to a fish tank that sported a Caribbean backdrop, coloured gravel, and a grotesque plastic shipwreck, but seemingly its residents must have found waters new which reminded me of the escaping fish in *Finding Nemo*. I whispered as much to Tam, knowing Disney films to be a safe topic; we laughed but there was a forced jolliness to it. The day was getting to us both.

One of our charming hosts came over with our order, white stoneware cups sliding on the tin tray, coffee slopping into saucers, that disappointingly looked nothing like the advert. I chided myself for my ungrateful thoughts, it was still coffee I supposed.

'Here you are then, girls. Can I get you anything else?' he enquired as he set down a disappointingly small bowl of stick fries and a token sachet of tomato ketchup, that were also nothing like what I had been expecting. I didn't look at Tam for fear it would encourage her to say what I suspected she was thinking, and opted out of replying myself by giving the lad my best smile and taking a sip of my coffee with the zeal of a drowning man grasping at a stick of wood.

The coffee was vile. Shocked, I managed to keep what I hoped was an expression of gastronomic delight upon my face while Tam thanked him politely. It had that cheap chicory flavour that reminded me of the Camp coffee, all that was affordable during the coffee shortage back in the mid-seventies. Caution thrown to the wind, I took the paracetamol out of my pocket and popped two from their silver pockets into my hand.

'Headache?'

'Mmmmm, not too bad though.'

'Me too, can I have a couple?' I passed the strip across. This was not how I wanted to remember my last day; I tried again to re capture our holiday mood, grabbing at the topic uppermost in my mind.

'The 'Englishman's house was amazing though, wasn't it?'

She said nothing for a while, studying my face intently, unusually, considering her reply.

'Yes, it was. But think about it, Mum... Is it right for you? What if you fall over, or your heart fails, or something? How would you get help? There's probably no phone signal there, and no one would hear you calling. You could be rotting before anyone found you, and it's not like any of us are going to be able to get to you easily. What would you do...?' She paused to take a sip of her coffee...God this is awful.' She grimaced, adding several spoonsful of sugar which she didn't normally take.

'What *are* you going to do when you *really* get old, and can't manage anymore? I opened my mouth to say

Coffee, Chips and Harris Tweed

something flippant but didn't because I could see she was serious.

'I don't know' I said instead. Almost a whisper, noticing the dark specs in her coffee as she stirred to fill the silence.

'I'll look after you,' she said eventually. 'I'll come up here if I have too... Just no bloody goats. You must do what's right for you... but it's going to be fucking cold in the winter.'

We didn't speak much after that. I was disappointed with what was supposed to have been a final celebration and stumped along behind Tam after we left the café, not even in the mood for the tweed exhibition. We both just wanted to get the long journey home done with now that our time here was over.

But, as we walked back past the bag shop, I made a decision, and did what my mother used to accuse me of quite frequently, *I dug my little toes in.*

'Stubborn as a donkey' she used to say in despair. I was not going any further until I had taken just a wee peek at the bags.

Noticing me again, the shop assistant came over and ushered us in out of the wet. I explained I wanted a bag... Her colleague who had been folding scarves joined us, and a woman sat behind the counter making good use of her Hijab to modestly feed her baby joined in too. I had narrowed the choice down to two. A browsing customer suggested that the brownish tweed echoed the dormant heathers and exposed peat, as it was now, so a fitting reminder of our holiday. The other popular choice was heather mix, as it was more fun, with the added benefit that it complemented the scruffy old dog-walking coat that I was wearing.

Tam noticed me struggling with my financial conscience and offered to pay some towards it as a thank you. I was reminded of myself with my own mother on the Australian visit, twenty years or so earlier. Mum hadn't spent anything on herself the entire visit, but I could see she wanted an opal ring, gleaming from a jeweller's window, in Gisborne.

When pressed, she confessed that she had known that Australia was famous for its opals and before leaving home had thought she would buy one as a souvenir. But she hadn't realised they would cost so much and there was no way that she would spend so much on herself. *We are so alike,* I realised warmly.

I had paid towards it just as Tam was doing for me now, a generation later. The camaraderie of women transcends generations.

I got my bag, going with the fun colour choice, that I thought Mum would also have chosen, in memory of our Australian trip. Its stiff smartness made my coat look even shabbier, but I was delighted with it.

Moods lightened, I skipped around the Tweed exhibition with a lighter step and making our way to the airport, I chewed over the potential for an Englishwoman, such as me, with just a little experience, weaving for the Harris Tweed Authority in her own shed, from a little croft by the edge of a loch… It was a pleasant wonder. The sun was shining again.

32. The Mists Clear

I got home just before midnight, after dropping Tam in Okehampton. I'd opted to carry on back to Cornwall, glad of the night's silence to sift through the turmoil of my thoughts. The conversation in the café had raised some awkward truths. I countered with myself that this was my last chance to do what I had always wanted, I just couldn't let it go, but at the same time, I was frightened that I had already left it too late. Was 'just me' enough? Did I even know who that person was yet, let alone what she really wanted, or what would make her happy?

What would I say to the sixteen-year-old me, with fantasies of her long hair, wild and free, curled by the mists of the machair? The nineteen-year-old me, who imagined children sitting around a scrubbed-top table after school, munching on fresh-baked cookies telling her about their day at school? The romantic naive young woman, who believed her husband would adore her, greet her with a kiss when he came home from work while she stirred something tasty on the stove. What would I say to them now?

I was always smiling in those daydreams, and I cursed myself for my idealism: *'head in the clouds,'* as Mum was fond of telling me. What an idiot I had been for so much of my life. As I negotiated the numerous gear changes needed to navigate the twisty lanes over Bodmin moor, every wrong turn I had ever taken in my life took turns to confront me. By the time I pushed open the back door to my lonely house, I felt too broken to fix.

My depression lasted a few days until I had caught up with my sleep, and something like the old, optimistic me returned. I was no nearer knowing what to do about moving, but *'sitting around moping never did anyone any good',* as Mum would also have said. So many times, I had proved that to be so.

I took my battered copy of *The Hills is Lonely* from my still-packed suitcase to put it back with its friends on the shelf, fondly acknowledging the scars of its long association with me. A strip of masking tape now held the front cover in place and the first few pages fluttered to the floor as I picked it up. My name hugged the very top edge of the fly sheet, as if apologising for defacing the brand-new book it had once been. The letters, formed in the same small, neat hand as the writing on the back of the Skye photograph taken the same day. The day of the dream's inception. My writing has the look of a pupil anxious to gain favour, but there is rebellion in the way that, unrestrained by the lines of a school exercise book, the V of my first name is completed by a firm elongation to the upward stroke, like the wings of faraway seagulls in a watercolour painting. A hint of the self I would grow to be.

I tapped the author's name into the search engine on my phone. I had devoured these books, but realised I knew nothing of the author who had penned them. What did 'semi-autobiographical mean exactly? With a sinking heart, I read on to discover that *Lillian Beckwith* was a pseudonym, her real name being Lillian Comber, and although she had lived on the Hebridean Island of Skye, it wasn't as the hapless Miss Peckwitt with her lovable caricature of a landlady Morag, but with her husband Edward. This was a shock. I had

The Mists Clear

never considered the stories to be anything but real. This rattled my faith. It was like finding out that Santa's reindeer cannot fly. Worse, it seemed that Lillian Comber's thinly veiled descriptions of her neighbours caused such offence that she eventually felt compelled to leave the islands for the Isle of Man, where she lived until her death in 2004 – the year I had first stayed with Roland and Debbie, and my first experience of The Isles of Lewis.

'Life isn't like it is in books you know'.

I whistled the dogs and pulled on my wellies. I realised my dismay was totally irrational and unreasonable. Ms Comber was just like any other writer telling a story. I was the one who had the problem. 'BUT' I told the loping backsides of the hounds ahead of me, 'being positive, the book was based on her experiences around 1950, *obviously* times would have changed since it was written... the islands had changed in the fifteen years from my first visit. BUT' I continued to my unresponsive audience, 'elements of Miss Peckwitt's life can still be retrieved, even if the hills were not quite so lonely now. This is not a set-back, it is an awakening: I don't need her anymore.' The dogs carried on, apparently not having an opinion either way.

When I got back, as if to emphasise my coming of age, I found a green felt pen that still had some life left in it and underneath the signature of the Viv the dreamer, I scrawled my name in big girl writing and firmly drew a line under it. I was back. Reindeer may not fly but Christmas can still happen. It was time to talk seriously with the family.

'I know it sounds mad, being up there all on my own…'

'Who says you'll be on your own!' interrupted Robin, with a wink of camaraderie. We laughed. I knew he would love it too. It was mad. I wanted it to be mad. I wanted to fall into bed at night exhausted but pleased to have made use of my skills. To know I have survived because of me. More importantly perhaps, one last crazy thing before I put the blanket over my knees.

The little croft on the shore was calling me. I had no illusions: the 'Englishman's' hideaway was a place that would tolerate no half measures. It would either be the most amazing thing I ever did or the biggest disaster of them all, but I wanted to try. So, I set the wheels in motion to sell my house. To offset the lunacy, I demonstrated being sensible by emailing Layla at the Hebridean Estate Agency, to ask about the access across the moor to the 'Englishman's' house. Could I use a quad bike, for example?

Days passed into weeks as I waited for a response. I started planning my route with the help of Roland's handwritten instructions from 2004. But no one seemed to want to help me, emails went unanswered, phone calls passed me around in circles; I was getting nowhere. Perhaps it wasn't meant to be after all? Then, amid all the stalemate, I got an offer on my house.

I was sat at my desk in my spare bedroom at the time, looking out over the sea on one of the best of early summer afternoons. I felt reckless. From the window, I could see playful sunlight on the waves rippling beyond the fading stripes of the hay field.

Heart thudding in my head I picked up the phone, calmly adjusting the volume to deafening-for-most-

The Mists Clear

people as if in slow motion. I tapped in the number carefully, and waited, feeling as I had felt all those years ago, waiting for the call to tell me I had my land, until a lilting Gaelic accent answered.

I told the solicitor to stress to the vendors that I *do* want to live there... No, it won't be a holiday home... She laughs, I laugh, I feel she is on my side.

'Leave it with me,' she says, 'I'll get back to you.'

To keep busy while I waited, I made a start on clearing out the shed. I thought it could be a while before she rang back, indeed if ever, but I was wrong. I had barely made inroads into the shed when the phone rang.

'I'm sorry but ...'

And there, stood among the tins of half used emulsion, I was told that an offer had already been accepted. The house was sold. MY little croft on the shore was going to belong to someone else.

'But it's still for sale on the website...' I stammered, 'I've been checking every day'.

'They do apologise for that. They accepted the offer two weeks ago. They just hadn't got around to taking it off.'

'I can't believe it,' I said, bewildered. 'It's been on the market all this time, years... and someone else decides they want it *now*?'

'I am very sorry... but there's nothing I can do.'

It wasn't really morning, but I couldn't stay in bed any longer. I had to get outside. I needed the fresh air and space to help me think things through. My tiptoeing attempt to slip quietly out of the front door and not disturb the dogs was scotched by having to tussle with the handle of the front door, stiff with disuse and the salt in the atmosphere.

Meanderings of a Serial Goat Keeper

In the days since my hopes had been so viciously dashed, I had scoured the estate agents for another Hebridean idyll, but there wasn't one. Prices had rocketed, even in the last few months, and there was nothing I could afford that was remotely habitable. To help me feel better I had allowed myself to acknowledge the disgruntled rumblings I was seeing on Facebook too. Niggles about tourists turning up without booking, inconsiderate parking, litter, and posts about their young people having to leave for the mainland because incomers were taking their houses seemed to be frequent. Problems that didn't exist in Lillian's time, but something that was very familiar to me in Cornwall. I was realising that the two places have so much more in common, than just stunning scenery and Celtic heritage.

This new reality was at odds with my romantic notions based on Lillian's books and hard to grasp. My dream was like a friend who had always been there, it was part of me. It had shaped who I was for nearly fifty years. Without it, who was I and how did I look forward?

It took about ten minutes to walk down the hill to the beach. I saw just one solitary hiker, striding purposefully out of the sea-mist, his walking poles marking his footsteps.

'Mornin',' I nod as we pass.

'Going to be nice later.' I see him reply. The tide was going out I realised, pleased as it meant that I could scramble around the rocks to my favourite cove away from the main beach. There was a dog walker at the far end, but otherwise I am left alone with my thoughts.

The hiker was right, there is a hint of brightness to the east where the sun was doing her best to push aside her

The Mists Clear

duvet of cloud. I made myself comfy on a dryish patch of shingle to the lee of one of the purplish rocks.

The air felt damp, tasting of brine, and the unmistakable smell of rotting seaweed was hard to ignore, but I closed my eyes and tried to untangle my thoughts by throwing them out to the waves.

It was a good place to sit. Typical of many in Cornwall, the natural harbour was cupped by the headlands either side, making it a great choice for local smugglers of old, who knew where the malicious rocks lurked that caused the grief of the many that didn't. Legend has it that a French trawler, the 'Marguerite' had floundered here almost a century ago. Her remains were supposed to lie somewhere on the seabed still, her boiler visible on the rocks at low tide, but I had never seen it. I assumed it must have been washed away long since.

I sat there for a long time. The waves left rockpools in their wake, small crabs scuttled for shelter, and crimson-haired sea anemones swayed to the rhythm of the sea. Limpets gripped tighter to the spot to which instinct would always guide them back to await the return of the tide. Minutes, maybe hours, had passed while I thought about life, the Universe and… death. As the years passed more quickly, so the people who died got closer in age. From dusty old relatives, then my parents and almost an entire generation of uncles and aunts, the old retainers of the goat world who had advised me when I first started… all gone, and now the ones my age were going too. Recently a school friend. Someone I had sat with in class, shared lessons with, and moaned about the same grey, lumpy mashed potato for our dinners. In my uncertain world, the one certainty I do have is that there are fewer diaries waiting for me to write than ones I have already written. I needed to think carefully about what was left for me.

The sun was getting more confident now, its fuzzy glow lightening the clouds. I supposed I should get back to my dogs. They would be wanting their breakfast. I stood and shook out my stiff legs, noticing that the beach behind me had filled while I was lost in thought. The tide too had turned, and I would have got a wet backside if I'd stayed there much longer. I felt more optimistic about the future. I wasn't sure if I had found any answers, but the bay had worked its magic and restored my faith, and belief that the universe knows what it is doing, even If I don't. I felt like me again. I knew I had so much to be thankful for.

As I turned to go, my eyes were drawn to a knobbly, cylindrical, rust-coloured object at the end of the rocks. I scrabbled over the rock-pools to get nearer, earning a wet foot in the process, but I thought I knew what it was. A tingle shivered through me. I was looking at the boiler of the 'Marguerite'. The very thing that I had so often looked for but never found.

The sun chose that moment to push its way through, and the mists cleared.

Like all first loves, the Western Isles will always be special to me. At least Cad had made it there, and his legacy lives on. I will always have that connection. But today, the rusty old boiler of a stricken ship taught me to trust in the rhythms of nature and to have patience to wait for the time to be right. As Mum used to say, *'Your turn will come'.* I just hoped it was better at navigation than me.

The Mists Clear

And goats...? A peep under the abundant foliage of the tumbler tomatoes hanging from the fence in my garden, and at the hook-over supports for the large terracotta pots where strawberries are ripening, will reveal hay racks and goats feed bucket rings... It wouldn't take much to tip that lot out.

...The sun is melting over the hills
All our roads are waiting
To be revealed
For this day in history has brought us to here
Now it's all there for the taking
The day is what you see...

Runrig

Writers: C & R Macdonald
BMG Publishing

Acknowledgements

Heartfelt gratitude to all who have supported, encouraged, and cajoled to get this book written.

To Debbie and Roland of Cappanuke goats for their care of Cad, for such generosity, thoughtfulness, and for allowing me to use the image of Cad for the cover.

The lads from Runrig for their kind permission to use the verse from Maymorning (In Search of Angels 1999).

Especial thanks to my patient friends and family who have been there with cups of tea when most needed. Without you I would have no story worth telling.

About the Author

Viv's still dreaming of the Hebrides, but also follows the family's dogs around the craggy coastline of Cornwall, the Moors of the South West, and the softer undulations of Devon. She is still a member of The Devon Goat Society and The English Goat Breeders Association and has many goatkeeping friends tolerant of her goat fix requirement. Any odd moments are spent writing, reading, and exploring various crafts, especially woolly ones, or trying to encourage things to grow in in the salt laden air that blusters over her garden.

God

The Way

I Am

Jim Ryan

Copyright © 2023 Jim Ryan
Cover Layout Teri Crawford
All rights reserved.
ISBN: 9798392423088